The

Budanest

Gareth

Hutchins

Thanks:

I'd like to thank my pygmy mother for her tireless effort in bringing this book to life. Without her as the driving force, and her loyal sidekick Tony (aka Head of Proof Reading), this book wouldn't have seen the light of day for many a moon.

I'd also like to thank Denes and Marta for being there so often to help during our most sleep-deprived moments of parenthood. You're both clearly insane. And I'd also like to thank Mila, the real star of the show. Our beautiful, blonde-haired, blue-eyed, tiny, dancing, little lunatic. You're one the funniest humans I know and without you his book would only be a pamphlet.

And last, but certainly not least I'd like to thank my beautiful boutique wife, Zsuzsa. Thanks for being so wonderful, so inspiring, for being my translator extraordinaire and for somehow managing to squeeze a human out of your bits. I love you and I'm sorry for publishing a book that talks about your perineum so often.

Te vagy mindenem x

For Mila, Lola & Zsuzsa

The Prologue

I live in Budapest. This is very odd as I don't usually live in Budapest. In fact, I've never lived outside of the UK, but here I am, sitting on a sofa in my new digs in sunny Budapest. A soon to be forty-year-old, soon to be first-time father, immigrant. My heavily pregnant wife is currently on the phone, speaking to her mother in tongues. Some Hungarian duck pate is lazily lounging on a piece of Hungarian bread on a table next to me. All of the food products in our kitchen have an unnatural number of 'Zs' on their packaging. If I look up, my view is of the Buda hills. It's sunny and hot outside! No, this is definitely not London in June (which according to the grumbles and moans that I've read via Facebook is currently suffering rain on a biblical scale). I arrived two days ago and still feel very much like an old cat, torn from his natural habitat and dumped into a new home. I'm discombobulated, sniffing all of the new corners of my home whilst resisting the urge to pee and mark my territory. What am I doing here?

Well as all good stories should begin, it started with a brain fart.

"What if we move to Budapest for the first year of Junior's life?".

We initially dismissed this thought, but soon realised that it wouldn't simply dissipate like a well-behaved fart into the ether, no matter how vigorously we wafted.

Naturally there were opposing thoughts that did their best to put us off the Budapest scent. "What about my job? What about our mortgage? How would we watch Masterchef?" But then that little brain fart slowly became a brain hurricane, battering all obstacles in its path and turning the opposing thoughts on their heads. "What if I quit my day job and pursued my dreams of being a full-time writer? Why don't we rent our place out? We can stream Masterchef via the old tinterweb can't we?" And so I did it. I quit my lovely, secure day job in London and we found renters for our London basecamp. What followed were several weeks of blind panic. I'd wake up in the dead of night, mind racing and heart pumping. My thoughts during these wee hours usually went along the lines of...

"Fucking hell! What in the name of God have I done?! I won't have a job! Nobody will understand me! I'm going to be forty! I will be forty seven when my child is seven. But that's only three years from fifty! When I'm fifty, that's only ten years from sixty! I'm supposed to retire at around sixty five aren't I? I'm a mere half a century from the probable end and I've just quit my job to go and live in a country where they speak mostly in 'consonants' and I have a baby on the way! Help me!"

But with the unwavering support of my miniature wife, my tiny tower of strength, I got through those dark hours, and now here I am in beautiful Budapest, trying in vain to understand what on earth everyone else is saying, whilst eating an unnatural amount of sour cream and with a heavily pregnant little lady by my side. The next 12 months or so should be an interesting ride, full of cultural clashes, sleepless nights, shitty nappies and me being a clueless father in a foreign land. So like a slightly more hirsute Captain Jean-Luc Piccard, I'm going to chronicle my adventures. Here we go...

Day 1

Chapter 1

It's my first full day in Budapest. I wake up, the sun is shining. Yes! Take that UK! Shove your erratic weather right up your rainy anus! My heavily pregnant Hungarian wife, who at this late stage of pregnancy is beginning to resemble a pregnant guppy, is in the kitchen making coffee. I step out on to our little, but delightful, balcony and survey the scenic Buda hills, take a great big contented breath of Buda air, and then it hits me. Bloody hell, it's hot! Very hot. I immediately make a calculated decision that it's too hot for pants and this, obviously, makes me happy.

"Morning honey" my miniature wife beams, waddles over with her big fat belly full of baby, and hands me a piece of paper with an unusual number of 'Zs' on it. I look at the paper, puzzled. "This is your list of challenges for the morning". Have I woken up in The Crystal Maze? As wondrous as that sounds, alas the answer is no. I've been given a number of 'The Apprentice' style challenges to complete, assuming of course, that it was an episode of 'The Apprentice' where they were challenged to go and buy nectarines. The thing about me, probably one of your favourite bits about me actually, is that I'm bloody brave.

"I accept your challenge! I will buy you fruit!"

And so off I trot, to the wild plains of Buda, a warrior in flip-flops, armed only with a piece of paper covered in 'Zs' and a mobile phone with a dodgy reception. Shortly after stepping outside I notice something unusual about my hair. It has become apparent that my hair and the Hungarian climate are an unusual, dare I say it, heady mix. Back in dear old Blighty my hair is slightly wavy, but nothing too extravagant. However, after a little under five minutes in the mid-thirty, Hungarian heat, my hair has decided enough is enough and is making a play to become exceedingly extravagant. My hair has turned into Liberace. Suddenly I'm a white man with an afro, or so it feels. I need to check this bad boy out before meeting my friendly local greengrocer who I'm sure, even before meeting him, is called Laszlo.

Being the eagle-eyed swine that we both know that I am, I spot a darkened car window just a few metres ahead and on the other side of the road. Bingo! I momentarily wonder if there are Bingo halls in Budapest and then flip-flop over to the car, looking around to avoid appearing like a preening, vain peacock wearing a David Hasselhoff wig. With the coast seemingly clear I peer into the dark, back seat window and begin inspecting the damage. Verging on a code red, curly hair disaster, but I can manage this. With a bit of spit and a fleshy five pronged comb I can tame this frantic beast. And so I set to work.

You know how when you're in a lit room and the lights go out, and for a few moments everything is pitch black, but then gradually, your eyes adjust and you start to make out shapes? Well the same is actually true for darkened car windows. I'm leaning right in, staring so intently at my own reflection that I can count my own pores, when something moves. It's in the car. I adjust my gaze slightly and then lean in further to inspect the movement. What I see chills me to the core. There's somebody starring back at me. A pair of eyes. A startled pair of eyes. A startled pair of female eyes. A mother's eyes. A breastfeeding mother's eyes! I am staring intently at a breastfeeding mother, discreetly feeding her tiny baby. Oh, the horror! And yet I'm still staring, like a rabbit caught in the headlights! Must...stop... staring! The expression on the woman seems to be changing. Anger is replacing fear! I do the only sensible thing that I can do. With all of the blood drained from my face like a piece of halal meat, I mutter the word "sorry" under my breath, turn and hurriedly canter away, flip-flops clopping like a mule.

Back in the safety of the flat, moments later, I tell my wife the bad news.

"All out of fruit, sorry honey".

The streets of Buda are fraught with peril. The next twelve months could be dangerous.

Day 2

The Sausage

I've been in Budapest for two days now and I fancy a sausage. As luck would have it, I'm standing outside a shop on Szent Istvan Kerut that looks suspiciously as though it may contain sausages. I wander inside and intrepidly make my way through the shop. Aisles of tinned food, bottles of potent spirits, fresh tomatoes, peppers and cheeses try to put me off the meaty scent, but they are doomed to failure. Nothing can stand between this man and his sausage.

I reach the back of the shop and I am delighted. For in front of my sparkling eyes lies some kind of sausage Babylon. Rows and rows of delicious, processed animal meat hang, delectable, delightful and practically screaming out to be devoured. "Come eat us!" they plead. "You are our destiny!" they somewhat creepily chant. But the path to my sausage destiny is not as simple as you may currently be imagining. Oh no! For I must first get past the sausage guardian who stands before me, behind a meat counter, guarding her meaty treasures. I am not fooled by her appearance. She may resemble a sweet, if slightly hairy, little Hungarian lady, but I know she is carved from granite with an unbreakable, iron will to protect these sausages from the unworthy. She has sworn an oath to these slender tubes of meat, and around here that means something.

Cautiously I take my position in a three person queue. Another elderly Hungarian lady comes and stands to my right and this throws me. Who is this brazen harlot, this free spirit, this renegade who doesn't abide by the law of the queue? Stand behind, not to the side! With my British upbringing, naturally, I am falling apart inside. While this battle is enraging, the leader of the sausage queue claims her meat and moves aside and the queue moves forward. Surely this challenger to my rightful throne will now hold back a step so that order can be assumed? But no! What is this treachery!? She moves forward with me, in unison! We are side by side! My mind is racing. Beads of sweat are forcing their way through the pores in my forehead. I'm sure I don't need to tell you that the next three minutes were some of the most stressful of my lifetime as this mental and physical battle took place. But, with a series of throat clearings, a subtle use of elbows and an ability to spread myself to three times my usual width, I eventually thwarted the challenger, despite her aggressive use of walking stick.

And now I'm at the counter, just me and the sausage guardian, face to face. But, then it hits me. I haven't chosen my sausage poison! I had been so engrossed in fighting off my queue challenger that I hadn't prepared myself mentally for my next challenge!

"Szia" bellows the guardian menacingly.

"Uh, szia" I skilfully retort.

"Kekndflsecnejnflzefmdzzwsnz?" apparently asks the guardian.

And in the heat of battle I panic. All of those Hungarian classes that I have been taking to prepare me for this epic moment are wasted. I can barely remember English. My queue challenger shuffles behind me, with menace. In that moment all I can do is grunt and point at one particular sausage adorning the wall. The sausage guardian looks at me and seems confused.

"Horz!" she says.

I have no idea what that means. I mentally travel back to my Hungarian class in London, racking my brain. No, 'horz' is a new word for me. I nod defiantly.

"Horz?" she says again, although this time adding a question mark.

The sausage guardian is apparently perplexed by my choice of sausage. Is this a trick? I need to be assertive and demonstrate that I am worthy of this treasure. I need to display my balls of steel (not literally). I compose myself.

"Igen, köszönöm szepen" I reply, suddenly delighted with my use of the native tongue.

The guardian, clearly impressed by my linguistical magnificence, but trying to play it cool, shrugs, grabs the sausage from its hook, wraps it in paper and hands it to me. I return the kind gesture by crossing the guardians palm with forint, turn and triumphantly leave. I have won. I am the penitent man! I have passed the test. I have seen off my challenger. I will now return home to my basecamp, present my heavily pregnant wife with the fruits of my victory and we will enjoy sausage!

Thirty minutes later.

"Honey. Why have you bought a horse sausage?"

We order a pizza.

Day 6
Radio Fame

Today I was interviewed by one of Hungary's biggest national radio stations about the Brexit. And this is unusual as in my six days living in Hungary I have hardly ever been on the national radio. So when I was contacted by the radio inviting me to share my thoughts, I decided to break my ominous radio silence and the whole of Hungary breathed a collective sigh of relief.

"Would you prefer to speak in English or Hungarian?" I was asked. I pondered this dilemma for a few moments before deciding that I'd probably struggle to get my succinct political thoughts across using only the four words of my Hungarian vocabulary. Especially seeing as one of those is 'paradiscom' (tomato) and another 'fogotmos' (to clean ones teeth). You can listen to the full interview online, but if you find yourself struggling to understand the Hungarian translation that has so rudely been placed on top of my sweet voice, it roughly translates as "Bollocks! That's me fucked then!"

It's crazy to think that I was the glue that kept the UK together. Of course, I'd always expected that this was the case, but it was only once I actually left the country and witnessed its catastrophic collapse into chaos and parody from afar, that my instincts had been proven right. We've voted to leave the EU, the prime minister has resigned, the candidates to replace Cameron remind me of the end of the film

Ghostbusters when the heroes were asked to choose their destroyer. Scotland might bugger off and they might take Northern Ireland with them. The inhabitants of Hull have all turned blue.

Pretty soon we'll undoubtedly run out of petrol and be ruled over by Immortan Boris. The next thing to go will be the food and we'll have no choice but to become cannibals, or something much worse…vegans. But I'm afraid I can't come to the UK's rescue on this occasion. I'm out here for at least a year now and have a miniature wife and an even more miniature baby to think of, so the UK will just have to pull itself together and get on with things without me

I've decided that I won't let fame change me. I may be Hungary's hottest new radio celebrity, but I have to keep my feet on the ground. I have a young family to think of. I won't go down the same route as the Justin Biebers and Kim Kardashians of this world. You might be sceptical of this, but I promise you, I won't.

But anyway, I imagine you're currently trying to work out what a Hungarian radio celebrity does to distract himself from the shitty mess that is The Brexit. Well, the answer is: get out of the city and enjoy some of the delights of Europe's largest lake. I am of course talking about Lake Balaton. So, we're now jumping in our Skoda Yeti hire car and will shortly by cruising down the M7 like some kind of Hungarian P-Diddy and Jo-Lo, Petofi Radio blaring out 80's Hungarian hits as we go, in a desperate attempt to forget all of the chaos in my homeland.

Day 35

Waiting for a Girl Like You

Speaking as a man who is yet to witness a baby tearing his wife's perineum apart with just its head, I think it's the waiting that's the hardest part. We've been on tenterhooks for two weeks ever since the doctor remarked that the baby could come at any minute, but so far 'nada'. We can't go too far from base camp, I can't drink booze despite being surrounded by delicious Hungarian grape juice wherever I turn. So we just sit and wait and when we're not sitting we're walking. In fact, we've probably covered every yard of Budapest in the last week. Which when you consider that my wife has to carry her belly in her arms, is quite a feat. Across streets, over bridges, to fröccs and langós festivals, over hills, to a Picasso exhibition, through markets and even to a concert (Budapest Bar) she has carried that gigantic belly in her tiny arms. She may look like an Easter Egg with legs, but I have to admire her pluck.

But anyway, I've now been in Budapest for about a month and I'm with a friend at a small beer garden (Spiler) near Buda Castle. The friend has a two-year-old child and he may not yet realise this, but he is my Obi-Wan Kenobi of fatherhood. With Junior's arrival looming large I am looking for reassurance, guidance and a few handy tips of how best to keep a human cub alive. I'm also trying to assess just how tough the first few weeks of parenthood might be.

"You know the first couple of weeks with the baby?" I say.

He throws back the hood of his robe, leans upon his staff, looks me in the eye and then wisely replies, "Yes". This is good. So far, all positive.

"Will I be able to get any sleep?" I ask.

At this he laughs so hard that food comes out of his nose. I am surprised by this response. Mainly because he wasn't even eating at the time.

"I didn't get any sleep for the first three months!" he snorts. "You're going to be so tired that you won't be able to feel your bloody face!". He chortles. "Take my advice young padawan. Get as much sleep as you can now as you won't be able to sleep once the baby arrives! You'll look and feel like SHIT!".

Naturally, I am thrilled by these words.

"But still, I guess I should count my blessings that I don't have a 9 to 5 job at the moment. Right now every day is Saturday!", I remark, striving for an upbeat finish.

"As soon as the baby comes everyday will be a Monday!", he sneers.

I consider whether I need a new Obi-Wan, whilst wondering if my friend has ever considered a career as a motivational speaker.

Nevertheless I have tried to take this sagacious advice on board and have been attempting to hibernate as much as possible. For two weeks I've been half man, half dormouse, but as we reach the finishing straight it's not as easy as one would think to pop off to the land of nodsville. The reason being is that I have discovered that once darkness falls I now achieve an unnaturally high state of alertness. I am a cowboy sleeping with one eye open. A praying mantis poised to strike. A man shitting it that his wife is going to go into labour. I think this newfound ability stems from someone once telling me that babies are most likely to come at night. The 'apparent' reason being that our instincts tell us that as it's quiet, there's a lesser chance of predators being around. I think this sounds like 'utter bollocks' as surely more predators come out at night, but nevertheless my subconscious mind believes them.

It's two in the morning. My wife gets out of bed to empty her battered bladder. Like a ninja I sense her stirring. My eyes shoot open and I sit up in bed, like a meerkat on speed.

"Are you alright honey? What's up?" I ask, but before she can reply I am already wearing trousers and searching for the car keys.

"Need a wee." she wearily replies. My trousers are off and I am back in bed. But I cannot sleep as I am fully alert, heart pounding. About thirty minutes later I eventually begin to drift off. Then up she clambers. I'm awake again. I'm wearing trousers. She is weeing. Back to bed. Repeat every thirty minutes until dawn.

Come on Junior! Please don't take after your mother and be late. We're waiting for you!

Nearly being a father is tougher than I'd imagined.

Day 42
Running Out of Names

Our baby is now five days overdue and we can't decide on a name. If we were having a boy the name was long decided and agreed. Hugo Zoltan Hutchins! He would no doubt have been both a comic book character and a wizard. But little Hugo will just have to wait as, unless it's a boy with a micro penis, all evidence suggests that we are having a girl, and we are more than delighted with this.

"Why don't we call her Sonia?" my wife suggests. I almost choke on my yogurt, which I'm confident would have been a world first.

I show her a photo of the Eastenders character called Sonia and she gets my point.

"What about Uma?" I ask.

"Are you insane!?" she growls back.

I take this as a maybe.

This game of baby name tennis has been going on for months now, ever since our twelve weeks scan where we discovered that we were most likely going to welcome a little madam into our world. The drama is also heightened on discovering that you are not allowed to leave the hospital in Hungary until a name is registered! Yikes!

I decide that a run might help with the baby name idea

generation. I am also spurred on by the realisation that I may have to take my top off in a hospital in the next few days for some skin to skin action with a new-born baby.

It's midday and I am running around Margit Island like an unconventional English/Welsh gazelle. It's over thirty degrees Celsius and I am the living embodiment for the Noel Coward song, "Mad Dogs and Englishmen". I am now rather regretting my running decision.

Half way through I spot a leafy little exercise yard and instantly decide that this is a perfect excuse to take a break from my foolhardy run. I study the machines on display and make a calculated decision that the peculiar devise that allows you to swing your legs from side to side is probably the least taxing of all the available machines. After all, what more do you want from exercise than to relax? So on I hop and begin the bizarre routine of swinging my legs from left to right. It's in the shade and I start to smile as I feel my life-force returning. But then something dreadful happens. Something almost too ghastly to even mention. A man makes his way towards my machine, and as bold as brass, hops on to the section that opposes me and begins to swing his legs about. He is facing me, our noses are centimetres from one another. His breath is caressing my skin. I am horrified by this brazen display of disregard for the unwritten rules of personal space encroachment. But not unlike Theresa May, I resist the urge to immediately trigger Article 50 as, being British, the last thing I want this random chap to know is that I feel uncomfortable by his unbelievably close presence. So, with my heart composing it's own hard-core drum n' bass 'tune', and with every fibre of my being secretly screaming "What the fuck are you doing you scoundrel!?" I try and play it cool. This begins with a nonchalant scratch of my shoulder with my chin. It provides me with the perfect excuse to move my face into a safe zone. But I immediately realise that this is only a momentary respite as I can only scratch my shoulder with my scratching chin for so long without appearing to have descended into madness.

I need a new 'face safety' strategy. In a eureka moment it comes to me! I will study the ground for a while as though it is as fascinating as the ceiling of the Sistine Chapel! But it's no use. I can't continue to look at the ground for more than fifteen seconds for fear that this stranger will suspect that I am looking uncomfortable, and as a Brit, it is in my DNA that I must do all that I can to avoid this shame. I reluctantly decide that there's only one thing for it. I brace myself and then slowly, calmly and assuredly look straight ahead, into the eyes of my aggressor. Our eyes meet and it is horrible. If we both extend our lips we could probably kiss. And in this bloodcurdling moment I'm now afraid that this is what he has in mind, so I quickly glance at my wedding ring in the vain hope that his eyes will follow. But they do not. This bushwhacker is made of sterner stuff and will not be fooled by 'sleight of eye' tricks. I want to grab him by the ears, shake him and forcefully say "I don't know what you're used to around this neck of the woods you cretin, but in Britain we respect each other's personal space!" But it's no use. This man is a shameless bastard, plus I don't know the Hungarian for "neck of the woods". Or "cretin". Or any of the rest of it. So I look at the ground again.

Eventually, after what seems like an eternity, but was probably actually less than thirty seconds I decide enough is enough. You have won sir. You have won! I hop off the machine whilst whistling, trying to act as nonchalant as possible and involuntarily break into a peculiar display of lunges to help me appear so. I don't think it worked. I then run away as fast as my tired legs and shaken mind will carry me, a mentally broken Brit in a land full of foreign, personal space invading madness.

About a hundred metres down the road I spot a little stall, selling beer. I decide to stop. I remember that all of the world's greatest ideas are generated in a pub.

Day 46

In Utero

My wife has a theory that our baby is reluctant to leave the womb as she is worried about the current state of the sterling.

"I'm not sure that she's actually aware of the current financial crisis facing Britain", I say.

"But the pound is doing so badly against the (Hungarian) forint!", she worriedly explains. "It's not good!"

I'm still not convinced.

"What if my worries about the financial climate are being projected onto her?" she continues. I guess this makes a little bit more sense. Maybe.

I try to reassure her. "Look, babies are late all the time. Just because she's decided to hang around in your womb it doesn't mean that she's scared. Take it as a compliment. I'm sure lots of people would rather be in your uterus. It would be the perfect place to avoid reading headlines from The Daily Mail."

Just at this moment there's a noise on our terrace. My wife doesn't hear it, but I do, probably due to my newly acquired heightened sense of alertness. I pick up a pencil as a weapon and go and investigate. It's a pigeon. A dying pigeon, sitting on the floor of our terrace. I think how lucky it is for any prospective burglars that this is a pigeon and not a burglar, as this pencil has been freshly sharpened.

"There's a pigeon on our terrace." I say. "I think it's dying."

My wife appears by my side, munching her way through a pineapple (in a desperate attempt to get the baby packing).

"Yes. It's definitely dying." she confirms, before adding, "What are you going to do about it?"

"What am I going to do about it?" I fire back.

"Well, are you going to strangle it?" she asks.

"What!? No! Why would I strangle the pigeon? I'm not the kind of guy who goes around strangling pigeons willy nilly!" But it occurs to me at this moment, that I am the kind of guy who uses the expression 'willy nilly'.

Only seconds later, the pigeon breathes a dramatic last breath and then face plants firmly into the concrete. I am sad for the pigeon, but also incredibly relieved that I don't have to throttle it.

"What now?" my wife asks. She's full of questions today.

I think for a moment before replying, "I guess I'll put it in the bin."

I go to the cupboard under the sink where we happen to store all of our plastic bags/pigeon coffins. I peruse the options on display before spotting the perfect choice. The pigeon may have suffered a sorrowful death, but at least she will find peace in an ornate, see-thru Aldi carrier bag at the bottom of a Sulo bin. A tomb fit for a pigeon king. I make my way back outside and carefully place the dead pigeon into it's discount chain coffin, using a used orange juice carton as a makeshift prodding device to confirm death.

With the pigeon in the bag, accompanied by the orange juice carton, I leave the flat and begin my journey to the bin. I decide to use the lift as I'm feeling hot and lazy. The door is about to close when a foot appears, blocking the door's closure. It is our neighbour, an old Hungarian man who doesn't speak English.

I look at the freshly dead pigeon in the see-thru carrier bag and simply think, "Shit!". I have never shared this lift with anyone except my wife, but fate has chosen this particular moment to alter this statistic.

The old man gets in and smiles at me. I try to hide the bag, but it's too late. He has seen the pigeon. He looks puzzled. I frantically scroll through my brain to see if I know any Hungarian that can help explain my situation. I've been learning an hour a day for the last six weeks and I'm getting much better. Sadly though I haven't yet covered the topic of pigeon deaths and bin burials. Also, I really wish I knew the Hungarian for "I don't usually shop at Aldi." So I simply smile awkwardly, shrug my shoulders and say "Pigeon", loudly and in English. It is horrible, but at least we only have two floors to go.

On the first floor the elevator stops again, unexpectedly. Three smiling Hungarian women enter. They look at the strange Brit carrying a dead pigeon in a see-thru, Aldi carrier bag and their smiles drop.

I wish I was back in the womb.

Day 47
Mila Time

Ladies and gentlemen, meet Mila Juno Hutchins. Mila Juno Hutchins, meet the ladies and gentlemen.

So, she's out, and as a result I have a new found respect for women. THAT. WAS. BRUTAL! My tiny wife somehow managed to push out a 57 cm long, 8 pound 10 ounce baby. My little wife who can still comfortably shop at Baby GAP. I have to doff my cap to my amazing better half and also to the miracle of modern medicine, as if the events of August 4th had taken place one hundred years ago I've no idea how we would have got her out. But all is well and we are both in shellshock. Oh my God. What a day. What a lovely day!

It started at 05:00 with The Show.

My wife wakes me up.

"Honey, The Show has started!"

The Show! The Fucking Show! Sounds like so much fun doesn't it? Visions of jazz hands, music, dancing, can-can girls and maybe even a magic trick. But then my wife shows me The Show first hand and I can confirm that The Show is not as entertaining as it sounds, and probably wasn't written by Andrew Lloyd Webber.

The Show was shortly followed by a series of contractions that made my wife make noises that sadly, I don't think I will ever make her make. It's definitely happening. I calm my wife by charging around the flat screaming "Don't panic!" I am Corporal Jones from Dad's Army. We get in the car and off we go. Over the past month I've discovered that the roads of Budapest are particularly confusing at the best of times, but when you are driving along with your wife screaming in pain every 5 minutes, and me screaming "Don't panic!" I can confirm they are still fairly baffling.

We get to the hospital and I am surrounded by rooms of women screaming and groaning. They are no doubt either giving birth, watching pornography or watching The Walking Dead. I mentally decide that they are watching pornography.

We get into a room and it begins. Zsuzsa is in pain, crying and wailing. Given that she usually cries if she misses a train this isn't abnormal, but I sense this is more than a missed train. Call it intuition. I give her a piece of chocolate and start recording her with a video. She doesn't appreciate this. I stop recording.

What followed was like the opening twenty minutes of Saving Private Ryan, but for seven hours. I've never witnessed such savagery, such brutality. Oh the horror! THE HORROR! I felt as though I was starring in my own, foreign language version of SAW.

At one point, I was holding one of my wife's legs, a midwife was holding the other, one doctor was playing the slip fielder, while another big male doctor pressed down hard on my little wife's belly, trying to force the baby out with some kind of crazy Hungarian toothpaste technique! And all of this whilst not understanding a single fucking word of what anyone was saying! Throw in an exam paper that I hadn't revised for and take away my trousers and that's my nightmare! Right there! I had visions beforehand of casually sitting by my lady wife's head, holding her hand and whispering sweet nothings while the doctor did the dirty work, but I had no say in the matter. I was at the business end. I was in the trenches. I probably now have trench foot.

And now it's over and I can confirm that I've seen things you people wouldn't believe. Attack ships on fire off the shoulder of Orion. I watched C-beams glitter in the dark near the Tannhâuser Gate. Now I've seen a baby's head do unmentionable things. All of those moments will be lost in time, like tears…in…rain.

If you are not familiar with Blade Runner you may now be thinking that I've been over doing it on the nitrous oxide. Outrageously though, they don't have nitrous oxide in Hungarian hospitals! It was the whole reason that I got my wife pregnant in the first place! Livid.

But she's out. Both mother and daughter are doing well. Mother will hobble and sit on a rubber ring for a few weeks I'd imagine, but all is good. We are ecstatic. Our little family has just grown by 50% and she's gorgeous. I'm sure there will be tough times ahead, but for now, we are an overjoyed, mentally drained, tired, family.

I leave the hospital for the night while my wife and little Mila both try and work out how to breast feed. I'm now outnumbered by ladies, but I wouldn't have it any other way.

Day 51

Budabreast

If you'd told me several years ago that during the summer of 2016 I'd spend a whole morning, miming the action of pumping a tit to bemused-looking, elderly ladies, on the other side of Europe, I'd have been dubious. Today this happened.

I was traipsing around Budapest in a desperate quest for a breast pump. From shop to shop I travelled, like J.R Hartley looking for a book on fly fishing, but with more nipples. And you know what? Not one person in any of the shops spoke a word of English! What on Earth are they teaching these people in the breast pump selling schools of Budapest!?

The situation repeatedly played out like this.

I enter a pharmacy/medical supply shop.

An elderly, gruff Hungarian woman stares at me blankly.

"Beszél Angolul (Do you speak English)?" I say.

"Nem (No)" they reply.

Bollocks.

I do the only thing I can, and look them in the eyes pleadingly, whilst pretending to grab my imaginary tits and squeeze them.

Cue a furrowed brow from the gruff Hungarian lady.

My eyes become more and more pleading as my tit squeezing mime becomes more and more elaborate. On a few occasions they twig and answer me with a shake of the head. On a few other occasions they just continue to stare blankly. But, just like those man-hungry Mounties, I eventually get my man/breast pump.

My search was all in preparation for my ladies finally returning home to our Buda Nest. Mila was born four days ago, but due to the particularly savage nature of the birth, Mila ended up hurting her collar bone and my wife dislocated her arsehole (or something like that). So they've been kept in until now to recuperate. Mila also needed a blood test as she was apparently looking a bit pale. Thankfully the results came back positive, with the midwife concluding that she was probably looking a bit pale because she was half British! What the...!? But today was the big day. They'd been given the all clear! My little lady and my even littler lady were coming home.

The message to come and collect them comes through and I'm overjoyed, despite the fact that it might disrupt my evenings, which over the last four days have consisted of me, a pair of underpants, a sofa, The Olympics and a bottle of wine. I jump in the car and race across Budapest to collect my girls.

Once at the hospital it becomes apparent that we now have an abundance of possessions that must go with us wherever we go. In the past, when we've hosted friends with children I've always been incredulous or sneerful, or both (sneerdulous?) by the sheer amount of apparent 'shit' that they've hauled with them. Sterilisers, little tubs of slop, numerous wheeled contraptions, bags, more bags, a few more bags just in case. Now, even before our baby has arrived home, I cast my eye at our car full of 'stuff' and begin to calibrate their apparent madness. It was bursting at the seams with baby shit (not literally)! I make a mental note to do all that I can to stop this insanity in its tracks. We need to be the kind of couple who put our flip-flops on, chuck the baby in a baby bag, grab our passports and toothbrushes and head to The Amazon. This may be wishful thinking.

We leave the hospital and drive home. Mila screams from start to finish. On the straights I almost reach twelve miles an hour. After what seems like several days (but was in fact less than twenty minutes), we get home and it hits us.

What the holy fuckety fuck do we do now?

Day 54

Escape From Baby Alcatraz

I'm sitting at home watching Tunisia play Qatar at handball whilst a baby who can't pooh screams in my ear. There's been a lot of obscure Olympic sports watched to the soundtrack of horribly shrill, poohless baby shrieking over the last few days. Judo, fencing, table tennis, canoe slalom, trampolining, something called radial sailing. I am well and truly living the fatherhood/Hungarian Olympic coverage dream. Maybe this is what heaven is like. I'm hoping things will change moving forward, but week one of parenthood has been like when the mafia 'go to the mattresses' during times of gang warfare. We've hardly left the house all week for fear of detonating an explodable baby bomb.

As it stands, if Mila is conscious, the only way to stop her screaming is to stuff a nipple in her mouth. Sadly, mine appear to be dormant, so it's my good lady wife who has to be constantly on standby with an emergency nipple bung. But then, when the time comes to remove the nipple from our human cub's mouth, it's like removing a pin from a WWII hand grenade that you've found in your back garden. You don't know if the hand grenade is live or not, but if it is live, you can be sure that it will take your face clean off and leave everyone around splintered with shrapnel.

This nipple stuffing technique does seem to be fool proof, but it's pretty tough for my wife. "I'm like an industrial cow!" she says.

"I'm just here for milking. I don't think she's even seen my face! All she's interested in are my tits!"

Maybe Mila takes after her father.

"Ahh." I reply in my most soothing voice. "You're not an industrial cow honey. More like a lovely organic cow that has been well looked after by a loving farmer."

I think for a second, before continuing with my inspirational pep talk. "I actually like to think of you more as her favourite restaurant. And not just any restaurant! You're not a Wimpy for example. If anything you're like a lovely little, local, healthy restaurant. You're probably even gluten free!"

A thought hits me. I haven't seen a Wimpy for about twenty years. I'm now worried that they may have gone the same way as the dodo, the woolly mammoth or C&A.

"But I can't keep up with the demand!" my wife moans, close to tears as she nurses her savaged nipples.

But it's no use, I'm not listening. My mind is focusing on the potential extinction of Wimpy restaurants.

At that moment we are interrupted by the midwife knocking on our front door. It's now been six days since Mila last poohed, so we just want to check that everything is in working order. The midwife enters, prods her little belly, pushes her legs up by her head and then puts a thermometer up her rectum. Once she's finished fooling around we show her to our baby.

"I think she seems fine" the midwife tells us. "It's often the case that new-borns don't poop much for the first week or two of their lives if they're being breast fed. Keep doing bicycle exercises with her little legs, massage her belly and before you'll know it, you will have more poop than you can handle." The midwife then leaves, leaving us once again, with our poohless child.

"Maybe she'll never pooh" I say. "Maybe she's like The X-Men! Maybe the next evolution of the human race will be a pooh-free human! Imagine how freaked out Andrex would be! The shit would well and truly hit the fan in their HQ, perhaps for the last time!"

On Mila's eighth day on Earth we decide to put our pooh concerns behind us, and prepare to face our fears by leaving our safe haven. She wakes up at midday. My wife pacifies her with a nipple. Half an hour later she slowly removes the nipple. Huzzah! This grenade is not live! We carefully place our cute little sleeping daughter into her buggy, pop our flip-flops on and leave the flat. Twenty metres later, Mila wakes up. She apparently doesn't appreciate the fact that we didn't get her to sign off for our expedition. She screams. Our neighbours no doubt assume that I am butchering a piglet. We return home.

We are prisoners to our nipple obsessed little warden. We are in Baby Alcatraz. But never mind. At least we can now watch India play Lithuania at badminton.

Later that evening, whilst I am helping Mila do her bicycle exercises, something shifts and things start to move. It happens whilst I am looking directly into the eye of the storm. I don't think I will ever be clean again.

Day 68

Do Babies Dream of Baby Sheep

You know how I said before that it was the waiting for the baby's arrival that was the hardest part? Bollocks! The waiting was the easy bit, as you can see from my new top three list of the hardest things about having a baby, ranked from hardest to easiest...

- The birth. Horrific. Brutal. Savage. Basically like a Saw movie. (Shudders)

- 24 hours of a baby crying. Oh! My! God! Please sleep!

- Waiting for an overdue baby.

In fact, as unbearable as it seemed at the time, I actually miss the waiting part now! I mean, we love our baby, we are over the moon, smitten, and very rarely think about selling her on eBay, but I live in a beautiful city, it's thirty degrees outside and I don't have to go and sit in an office! I miss being able to just take a stroll up to Buda Castle with my favourite wife, pop into Pest for a bite to eat, or visit one of the city's many bars or cafes for a sociable drink in the sun.

Maybe I'm just feeling a tad bitter due to the fact that Mila spent yesterday (which incidentally was our third wedding anniversary) screaming at the top of her tiny lungs. FOR TWENTY FOUR

FUCKING HOURS! I think she's maybe going through that phase. You know the one. The phase where the ONLY thing that will stop her crying is to be carried around by her Dad while he sings the entire back catalogue of The Crash Test Dummies to her. The trickiest part of this is that I only know two of The Crash Test Dummies' songs. These being 'Mmm Mmm Mmm Mmm' and 'Afternoons & Coffeespoons', and out of these two songs I know a total of eight words from the lyrics, seven of which are in the titles. So, our anniversary evening consisted of me, with wild, bloodshot eyes, wandering around the flat carrying a baby, guessing the entire back catalogue of The Crash Test Dummies.

"She's asleep honey! Why don't you try and put her to bed?" my wife says.

I nod and then looking like a man carrying his life's work through a field of land mines, I carefully put my sleeping child to bed. Her peaceful, sleeping head touches the mattress. Her eyes shoot open. She glares at me and she is frantic. She screams. I pick her up.

"Mmm, Mmm, Mmm, Mmm, Mmm, Mmm, Mmm, Mmm, Mmm."

Repeat until my eyeballs bleed, while I consider if there's any feasible way to put our baby back inside my wife.

One other thing that hopefully one of you experienced parents out there can help shed some light on. Why is it that a baby will sleep through storms, sirens, violent political demonstrations etc, but if you step on to a squeaky floorboard, wide awake! Why!? What is this witchcraft, this black magic! A few days ago we went for a walk with

Mila in her buggy. It was some kind of National Hungary Day so there were celebrations all over the city. We'd just managed to get Mila to sleep by walking vigorously over a cobbled street, when up ahead we spot something that terrifies us. A parade of Hungarian bagpipe players coming our way! About fifty of them, all gleefully blowing into their abhorrent sacks! We've no idea what Hungarians are doing playing the bagpipes, but naturally, we are horrified. We look for an escape route, but it's no use. We are surrounded. So, with darkness in our hearts we prepare to walk into the bagpipe playing hell. And...our ridiculous little human didn't so much as raise an eyelid! Astonishing sleeping skills! We are delighted! We get home, she seems to be in a coma, we put her to bed, step on a floorboard that had just at this moment decided to become squeaky. Eyes shoot open. Scream. We are broken.

"You know our baby?" I ask the wife.

"I know her." she replies.

"Well, I think she might be a bit of a dick."

"Don't say that honey!"

"I'm sorry, but she has screamed for the entirety of our wedding anniversary, only stopping if I sing early 90's, obscure, Canadian rock to her! Not only that, but she seems to time her number two's for when it's my turn to change her nappy! You get a little splash of fragrant baby wee, I get stinking baby jalfrezi! What the hell is that about!? Like I said, I think she might be a bit of a dick."

"She's not a dick. She doesn't understand what's going on. She's going through something called a leap. She's just scared."

"Well, I hope you're right! She better be scared shitless!"

When we do finally manage to get Mila to sleep I often find myself staring at her, wondering what the devil she's dreaming about. I mean, what does she know? She knows the inside of my wife's uterus, she knows that breasts are delicious, and she knows a tiny section of Budapest. She'd be a rubbish 'phone a friend' on Who Wants to be A Millionaire. She probably doesn't even realise that the United Kingdom recently had a referendum about whether or not to stay in the European Union! Or maybe I'm wrong and she knows a lot more than she's giving away. Maybe she has been quietly absorbing the world around her over the last nine months from inside my wife.

Or maybe she's just dreaming about my wife's breasts.

Day 75

Boob Wars

A few days ago I discovered that ladies with milky bosoms across the globe are furious with me. The reason for this unbridled rage? Because I am so massively anti-breastfeeding...apparently. I am momentarily confused, largely because I didn't even realise that I was against breastfeeding.

I first became aware of this nipply rage when an old work friend contacted me via Facebook to let me know that I had popped up in some breastfeeding group that she's a member of. The members of the breastfeeding posse are spitting vitriol at this evil dad who for some reason has made it his mission to prevent ladies' nipples from entering the mouths of their little babies. Smack bang in the middle of the post that they are so furious about? Me holding a breast pump to my man-titty while looking gormless. Great! My first time as the face of something and they had to use *that* picture.

"How dare he!" they howl. "This makes my blood boil!" they cry.

I'm still confused though. To be honest, I didn't even realise that it was a thing. Are people really against breastfeeding? Nevertheless, I guess it's one thing off the old bucket list. Become the poster boy for anti-breastfeeding groups? Tick.

I investigate further and discover that it all came about due to an article that I'd written for The Dad Network. This article, which you can read online, has somehow been interpreted as a vicious attack on breastfeeding mums. I read it again to see if I'd accidentally slipped in a sentence about how breastfeeding mothers needed to be burnt at the stake, just in case, but I can't find anything. It's just a (hopefully) humorous tale about our shell-shocked first week as parents.

I browse the comments on The Dad Network's Facebook page and I'm stunned. It appears that I've inadvertently started a war between two extremist breastfeeding factions. There are hundreds of clashing comments between the extreme left (who seemingly want to breastfeed everyone) and the extreme right (campaigning for the extinction of nipples).

I try to get my wife's attention. "Honey?".

But it's no use. She's too busy breastfeeding. Damn that natural and beautiful act between mother and child!

I try again and this time it works.

"What's up?" she says.

"Honey, am I anti-breastfeeding without even realising it?" I ask.

"I don't think so." she replies. "I mean, do you find yourself getting worked up into a blind fury when I feed Mila?"

"Not really."

"Do you hate breastfeeding Mums?"

"Not at all. I mean sometimes I don't know where to look, but I think it's a lovely and natural thing."

"Then I would say you're actually a friend of breastfeeding mums."

"I thought so too!"

"To be honest," my wife says, "I doubt they've actually even read your article. They've probably just read the headline that The Dad Network added and gotten the wrong end of the stick".

Nevertheless, I'm now living in fear that on an innocent walk to the local shops to buy nappies for my baby, I will stumble across one of those infamous, deadly gangs of breastfeeding mums that you hear about on the news. The ones that hang out on street corners or in tunnels, looking to cause trouble. Probably a gang affiliated with the extreme breastfeeding terrorist cell who I have unexpectedly clashed with. I am living in fear.

Please join me again next week when I will be writing about why mothers should lose the right to vote.

Day 82

White Candy

My wife has been thinking.

"Honey." she says. "I've been thinking."

Told you.

"You know what having a baby reminds me of?"

I lie there motionless, eyes closed and mouth open, a bit of dribble slopping out of the side of my mouth. A sexier image, you will surely not hear of today.

"Like travelling on the 6:30am Ryanair flight to London whilst looking after a crack addict, EVERYDAY!" she replies. "You're standing in a Ryanair queue before the sun comes up. You're so tired that it feels as though your skin is about to fall off your body, and all the while, someone with manic eyes is pawing at you, pleadingly"

I nod at my wise wife. She's hit the nail on the head. I've been trying to put my finger on the feeling for a few weeks now, but I think this tiny, female, milk providing soothsayer has nailed it.

"All we need now is for some bastard to turn up at our front door selling scratch cards!" she adds.

I think what my wife's analogy is alluding to is that we are constantly tired and our baby appears to be going through cold turkey every two to three hours. She wakes up in a blind panic. She's frantic!

She's desperate! Only one thing will quench this furious desire. That thing being a nipple spurting milk. I haven't tried my wife's milk, but by the reaction of her one, sole customer, that's some good shit she's peddling!

A thought hits me. Maybe my wife should open a milk bar, like the one in A Clockwork Orange! It would surely go down like a house on fire in Shoreditch. They'd be arriving on their penny farthings and queuing around the block to sample, what I have no doubt, is seriously addictive stuff. But then I start to worry that my wife's lactation process won't be able to keep up with her customer's demand. I'm also worrying that there will be complaints to Watchdog that she is dealing a new, legal drug. What would its street name be? 'White Candy' maybe. We might need to buy a camper van and head out into the desert to replenish our 'White Candy' stocks. It sounds like a lot of work. I decide that I don't want that stress for my wife. It's at this moment in time that I start to realise that I'm suffering from delirium, brought on by sleep deprivation.

To be fair to our little girl, she does actually sleep through the night like a fleshy little log. The problem is, we don't. The reason being that Mila often makes a choking sound during the night that suggests that she can't breathe. Concerned by this, we speak to the doctor and he assures us that it's quite common. Basically she can't yet swallow properly so either milk, mucus or both often get stuck in her throat.

We are momentarily relieved until he adds, "You should keep an eye on her though as there is a chance that she can suffocate in her sleep."

Great. That's sleeping off the menu for the foreseeable future then.

But anyway, today I am getting a temporary reprieve from our 'White Candy' loving, wheezy little human cub. I have been given a green card by my kindly wife and I intend to use it wisely. I've now been in Budapest for more than two months, but I'm yet to visit one of the city's amazing thermal spas. Today is the day where I rectify this.

A couple of hours later and I'm entering a sauna at Budapest's ostentatious Gellert Spa. The sweltering heat hits me and I feel a tad faint, but I decide to battle on. In the sauna is one other gentleman. An elderly Hungarian man in tiny speedos that are struggling to contain his low hanging testicles. I sit down and he smiles at me.

"Jó napot! (Good Day)" he beams, seemingly delighted to have some sweaty company.

"Jó napot." I reply.

"Hogy van? (How are you?)" he enthusiastically asks.

"Jó köszönöm. (Good thanks)" I reply.

The elderly gent obviously detects an accent as his next word is "Deutsche?"

"Nem. Angol (No, English)" I reply.

"I speak a little English" he says.

I smile back before asking "How are you?"

This was my mistake, for this man does not realise that if a Brit says "How are you?" he doesn't actually give a rat's ass how you are.

It's just a turn of phrase. It's akin to saying "Hi". If anyone replies with anything other than the stock answer of "Good" we assume that they are insane and proceed to panic. Apparently however, if someone asks the same question to a Hungarian, it is an invitation for them to tell you their life story, as the man then launches into a gargantuan monologue about the last few years of his life.

He explains that he has just retired, but that he's not enjoying it and that he wishes he was still working. He's struggling to cope with so much free time. He then begins to tell me about his family. His daughter is recently divorced and it's causing the family much anguish. He then elaborates on this subject, by divulging minutiae about his daughter's marriage and why, exactly, it broke down. But I'm no longer listening. I'm close to death. It's nearly one hundred degrees celsius in this hell hole of a room and my life is flashing before my eyes.

I'm discovering that living off minimal sleep for two weeks is not a good pairing for a room that's so hot that it would melt Frodo's ring. I want to get out! I need to get out! But I'm British! To simply get up and leave halfway through this man's story might seem rude. I'm trying to assess my options. Do I get up and leave halfway through this man's story, or simply give up and collapse, here on the smouldering floor. If I get up and leave now, obviously I will need to leave the city for fear of bumping into this man again. I mean, he might give me a disapproving look! Alternatively, if I collapse on to the floor, the spa will probably need to find a spatula to scoop me back up off it.

I eventually decide that social embarrassment is probably

slightly more appealing than potential death, and I'm about to leg it, when the door opens and another elderly gent in x-rated speedos enters. The two men's eyes meet and they begin to converse. I see my window of opportunity and leave the sauna. I can feel my blood simmering and now know what it must feel like to be a live lobster in a pot of boiling water, whilst an older lobster with low hanging testicles tells you a sob story.

All of a sudden, an early morning Ryan Air flight with a crack addict doesn't seem so bad.

Day 89

The Meat Baby

On three occasions this week, my wife and my new-born child have conspired to make me look like a psychopath.

This psychopathic tale begins on a Wednesday (as all good psychopathic tales should). Mila is sleepy, having tanked up on draught milk straight from the fleshy tap (she can have some of the bottled European stuff later). We bundle her into her buggy, pack her carrying sling just in case the milky sedative wears off, and leave our nappy-strewn fortress. Our destination? A local Hungarian market. A place where moustachioed men go to sell their fruity, meaty and er, vegetably wares. We arrive safe and sound, sleeping baby in tow, but as ever, we are nervous. Nervous as we have been fooled into this comfort zone before. On various occasions of late, our baby has tricked us with her promise of being a peaceful, sleeping baby, and then BANG! She's awake. She's making a sound that I imagine a goat would make it it was being attacked with a cheese grater. People are staring. I'm mouthing 'sorry' apolo-getically and then we sheepishly flee. On this particular occasion though, so far, so good. But we remain sceptical. A few minutes later, my wife is perusing the aubergines when our worst fears are confirmed. Mila is stirring. THE BRAZEN CHARLATAN! At this moment in time she's only stretching, but we are all too fully aware of what this is. This is a teaser campaign. This is the calm before the storm. This is the beginning. This is Germany invading Poland. In a state of panic we bundle her out of her buggy and into her sling, a trick that sometimes works. Mila lets out a big sigh and closes her eyes. We've done it! I think of what might have been, if only Poland had had a big sling in 1939.

"Honey!" my wife whispers. "We need to be quick. Why don't you go and get the ham and bread?" I silently nod my approval at this excellent, time-utilising idea and push our baby-less buggy over to the meaty section of the market. Using a combination of pointing and grunts I successfully purchase a shed-load of (what I assume is) ham, pop it into the buggy and head to the land of bread.

The bread section is bustling with elderly Hungarian ladies. It's packed and I see no way through, but remembering our ticking baby time-bomb I decide that I need to be ruthless and so stride towards them with a plan to use my ham filled buggy as a battering ram. I soon discover however, that the battering ram isn't required. The elderly ladies see me pushing the buggy and respond with beaming, adoring smiles and cooing eyes. This must be what it feels like to be Tom Jones! They move to let me pass and I now feel like Moses parting the Red Sea, but alas, it's short lived and within seconds I am engulfed as they then all huddle around the buggy. I'm drowning as they all peer in. Seconds later and the smiles are replaced with a strange look. At first the look is hard to decipher, but I soon realise that it is the look that people give when they peer into a pram expecting to see a cute baby, but are instead confronted with some lovely ham. They eye me suspiciously.

Now don't get me wrong. I'm fond of ham. If I could only eat one animal for the rest of eternity, pigs would be right up there. But I'm not so fond of ham that I would pop it in a pram and take it out for a walk. My paternal feelings towards ham are at best, weak. But these ladies think otherwise, and sadly my Hungarian is not of a standard where I can explain the truth. I decide that bread is overrated and leave.

A few days later and the folks have come to visit from Spain. We have been to a restaurant. For the most part, Mila was well behaved, but half way through our mains our baby bomb goes off. My wife scoops her up in the sling and we begin our hasty escape. I'm following about thirty metres behind, pushing my wife's uneaten chicken kiev in the buggy. At some traffic lights, people stare and then edge away from me. I again look like a psychopath who has taken it upon himself to raise some meat.

It's now Saturday and we are hosting the in-laws. It's late, but we decide that a walk might be nice, and so off to Buda Castle we trot. Twenty minutes later and someone is again attacking a goat with a cheese grater. We quickly pop Mila in the sling and the wife and the mother-in-law wander off to calm our frantic baby. I'm left with my father-in-law and the buggy and we decide to stop off at a little bar. I carefully park the buggy by a table and we sit down. The waitress comes over. She gives us a strange look. It suddenly dawns on me that we are two men, in a bar, at eleven o'clock at night, with an empty buggy that I am currently gently rocking back and forth. We look insane.

I decide that I should wear the sling from now on.

Day 96

The Wolf of Budapest

I've been on a stag do in Dublin and I am unbelievably tired.

The first two days were craic- (not crack-) filled, but it's now day three and I just want to go home. In fact, I would trade in one of my testicles if I could be immediately teleported back to my sofa in Budapest, where I would then proceed to nod off whilst watching House of Cards with my ladies. Alas, my flight isn't until the evening (damn you Ryan Air!). We are staying in a squalid little hovel in an area of the city that's bursting at the seams with dodgy-looking council estates. For some peculiar, unknown reason our accommodation also constantly smells of sausages.

All of the other members of the stag party apart from me have been forced to check out already, so as it stands there are currently twelve tired, hungover men with luggage in my room. Some of the guys are sleeping on the floor, three others share a bed, one has been gazing out of the window for about two hours, while another makes some tea. We look like Albanian immigrants waiting for a phone call to say that someone needs some tarmacking. To make matters worse, there's a big Gaelic football match taking place today, meaning that it's the busiest day of the year for the city. The result being that we need to get to the airport five hours before our flight or risk not being able to get a taxi.

After five long hours sitting in a Burger King in Dublin Airport (I should have set up a Justgiving sponsorship page), I get on my flight, the plane is pointed in the direction of Budapest and off we go. I skilfully manage to avoid buying scratch cards, we land, and I depart looking like one of The Walking Dead and fighting the desire to simply drift off into a lovely coma.

I eventually make it home to our nest. I open the front door and my wife flings herself around me. She is beyond ecstatic to see me. I haven't been greeted with such boundless enthusiasm since I had a puppy as a child. The puppy often weed on me in joy. Thankfully I have toilet trained my wife to a slightly higher standard.

I sneak into the bedroom to say hello to my sleeping baby girl. I peer into the cot. I see two large, wild eyes glaring back at me through the darkness. Either my wife has swapped our new-born for a bushbaby or this little human cub has decided to tear up the night and day rulebook. That night I sob into my pillow as Mila screams. ALL. NIGHT. LONG.

Eventually, extreme tiredness takes over, the screaming becomes background noise and I fall asleep. A couple of hours later, I am awoken by an alarming smell. My hungover brain has a horrible feeling that it knows where this smell is coming from. I look to my wife for help, but she is nowhere to be seen. All I can see is a wild eyed baby, staring back at me from her cot.

Mila makes a noise which I think is baby for "Are you going to change me or what, you lazy twat!?"

Reluctantly, I decide that I have to do my duty and I cautiously lift my tiny baby girl out of her cot and take her to her nappy-changing table. Like a nerd carefully unpacking a new iPhone, I begin to remove her outer layers.

Oh the horror! THE HORROR! What's that coming out of the nappy? Is it a monster? IS IT A MONSTER!? Surely this filth has come from a darts player after a curry night in a Weatherspoons rather than from my sweet baby girl. It's gargantuan! Also, I don't know how, but she's even managed to shit on her chest!

Fighting the urge to wretch for risk of adding vomit to this already beastly mix, I set about the clean-up operation. I'm like The Wolf from Pulp Fiction, if the Wolf was incredibly squeamish, bad at his job and sweated Guinness profusely. The filth is on my hands, it's on her clothes, it's around her nipples, it's on the nappy changing table, its engulfing me!

At this moment my wife emerges from the bathroom, sporting a beaming smile. "Do you know who our baby reminds me of on her ID card?" my wife asks. Still covered in shit, I rack my brains for famous babies or babies that we both happen to know, but I'm struggling. My head is pounding and my brain is close to death. All I can think of is Ross Kemp. I shrug.

"Bill Murray!" she says. I have to admit, I wasn't expecting that.

"Her face. She has the same face as Bill Murray." she adds.

I stare at the face of our beautiful, seven week old little baby girl, covered from head to toe in shit and it hits me.

My wife has just ruined Ghostbusters.

Day 103
Happily Ever After

My wife is concerned that I'm portraying our baby and parenthood in a negative light.

"You're always going on about how tired you are, how much she cries, her poops, how she's always hungry." she protests. "She's a very good girl and you don't really get this across. And if you're not complaining about our baby you're poking fun at me! Sometimes I'm afraid to speak now for fear that it'll end up in your blog!"

I'm wondering if this is the right time to tell my wife that she has a beetroot moustache. She's just arrived back from a shopping trip, in which she purchased some beetroot juice (apparently it's good for breastfeeding mothers due to its iron content). Such was her furious thirst to consume said beetroot juice, she opened it in the shop and took a swig. That's when the moustache was spawned. She's been walking around town with a beautiful purple moustache ever since. She looks a bit like her Dad. I decide that now is not the right time.

"Sorry honey." I say. "I don't mean to give the wrong impression. I'm just not sure how interesting it would be to read about how Mila has been a very good girl. I'll bear it in mind though and try and at least finish on an upbeat note."

The truth is that Mila is a smashing little cub. We do have the odd wobble, the odd sleepless night, the odd evening when we are afraid to breathe for fear of detonating her, and the only music that I've heard for the last two months is from an album of Hungarian lullabies, but overall she's a wonderful little girl and by all accounts much better behaved than her Daddy ever was. Apparently I never slept and came perilously close on several occasions to being flung out of a window! So basically, despite my occasional moan we're blessed, overjoyed, couldn't be happier and these last two months have been a dream.

I hear a shriek from the bathroom. My wife has just discovered her moustache.

Later that day there's a knock on our front door. It's Mila's masseuse. That's right, she has her own personal masseuse. Who the hell does she think she is? Prince Charles?

While Mila has her knots kneaded and the stress removed from her miniature back, I look on with envy. I want my knots kneaded! Inspired by this, I call the local massage parlour and book an appointment.

A few hours later and I'm being escorted into the massage room. The masseuse, thankfully speaks a little bit of English.

"Take your clothes off, but leave your panties on and lie face down on that table." she says.

I decide that she is muddling her English as the alternative is that I look like the kind of guy who wears ladies panties under my civilian clothes. I remove my t-shirt and then my shorts. I look down at my underpants and my blood runs cold. I haven't thought this through.

Batman pants! I'm a forty-year-old father, about to be massaged by a lady that I've never met and I'm wearing my batman pants! Actually, I'm a forty-year-old father, about to be massaged by a lady that I've never met and I'm wearing batman pant that were bought for me by my grandma! I realise that I look ridiculous and now I'm feeling stressed.

There's a knock on the door and the masseuse re-enters. At least I assume it's the masseuse. I'm too embarrassed to show my face so I've decided that I'm simply going to bury my face in the massage table until this whole palaver is over. The old ostrich technique. Smarter than they look.

"Music?" the masseuse asks.

I grunt in approval.

At least we can now have some relaxing music to whisk me away to a far- away place. The masseuse turns on the stereo. What will it be? Some Mozart? Some Enya? Peruvian panpipes? No, it's The Lighthouse Family's Greatest Hits. Of course it is.

But I must confess that despite my ridiculous appearance and occasionally being sound-tracked by the 1990's musical duo, the masseuse knew what she was doing and the massage was wonderful. So in a break from tradition and to please my beloved wife, I'm finishing with a happy ending.

Get your minds out of the gutter people! I'm referring to the story.

Day 110
Lost in Translation

I'm sitting in a waiting room, waiting for a business meeting. After a few minutes, the lady who I'm meeting appears at the door with a beaming smile.

"Hi. I'm sorry, but I won't be giving you any pussy today. I'm a bit sick". she says.

I'm now worried that I've misread the agenda. I mean I'm all for being friendly, but that's the kind of greeting that you rarely get, even in Essex. I'm also not sure that my wife would approve. She's funny like that.

The meeting runs its course, and true to her word, I am given no pussy. Not even a little bit!

An hour or so later and I'm on the phone to my wife, recounting the tale of the friendly greeting.

"She meant 'puszi'! It's Hungarian for kiss!" she explains.

"So it's not a Hungarian custom?" I ask.

"This isn't Ancient Rome!"

"And you're absolutely positive it isn't to do with the fact that I'm having a really good hair day today?"

"She meant 'kiss'!"

I'm relieved as I have a few other business meetings scheduled for the next few days, one with a fairly elderly gentleman who smells of tinned spam.

"That's a very funny misunderstanding" I say. "It's definitely going in my blog."

"Don't put it in your blog!" my wife says. "If she reads it she will be mortified."

Later that evening my wife has a look on her face that suggests that something is wrong.

"What's wrong?" I ask.

"Nothing." she replies.

Shit. This mean's something is definitely wrong.

I prod and poke her until she eventually caves.

"You know your blog?" she says.

"I'm aware of said blog" I reply.

"How come you only ever refer to me as 'wife'?" my wife says. "Everyone else has a name. Mila has a name. You have a name. I'm just 'wife'."

"I don't know." I say. "I think I just called you wife in the first one and then continued to run with it. Would you like me to name and shame you?"

"I want a name." my wife says adamantly.

It's later that evening and Mila is having one of those nights.

We can't stop her crying for love nor money. My wife's well appears to be running dry and not even the trusty old dancing to AC/DC trick appears to be working.

We try the dummy, but she keeps spitting it out. As a side note, why don't they make dummies with elastic face bands? If they're good enough for party hats... By the way, you can have that one for free. I'll keep an eye out for you next year on Dragon's Den.

After several hours of nursing, comforting and "shushing", my wife eventually gets Mila off to sleep. I sneak into the bedroom where they're both lying. A lullaby is playing. It's a lullaby that we've heard thousands of times over the last few months, and it's starting to make me want to eat my own feet, just to take my mind off it.

"Shall I change the music?" I ask with pleading eyes.

"As long as it's gentle and quiet." my wife replies, barely audible.

I scroll through my iTunes. I find The Carnival of the Animals, a magical piece of classical music that you'd recognise from countless films. I turn the volume down to near silent and press play.

But my iPhone has other ideas. It quite fancies listening to The Beastie Boys at full volume. My iPhone is a despicable dick.

"LISTEN ALL OF Y'ALL IT'S SABOTAGE!"

Mila is awake.

Zsuzsa is livid.

There will be no puszi for me tonight.

Day 119
Carry on Budapest

There's an old man standing in our flat in his underpants.

It's our neighbour. He rang the doorbell a few moments ago and when I opened it the scantily clad gent invited himself in. He's trying to say something to me in English, but struggling to find the words. I think he's asking if the noise from a neighbouring flat is bothering us, but to be honest, the only thing that's bothering me at this precise moment in time is the old man standing in my flat in just his underpants and an open, extravagantly multi-coloured overcoat. He looks like Joseph from Joseph and his Amazing Technicolour Dreamcoat, if Joseph had recently divorced, lost his job and then turned to the bottle for comfort.

"Maybe, best if I speak to Zsuzsa?" he says. "I struggle for the English".

Zsuzsa, you may well remember, is the artist formerly known as 'wife'.

"Zsuzsa!" I bellow. "Our neighbour is standing in our flat in just his pants. Help me!" I want to add.

Then I remember. Zsuzsa is in her underwear in our spare bedroom and our spare bedroom is only a few yards away from our erotically dressed neighbour. She's trapped! I block our neighbour's path to prevent him getting an eyeful of wife while I try and work out a plan. Moments later though and Zsuzsa confidently appears. She's wearing a large ski jacket (the only thing to hand). She walks up to our neighbour and I leave them to it. Just two people having a chat about a nearby Austrian oboe player. One wearing saggy white underpants and a coat made from the skin of butchered teletubbies, and the other a ski jacket in a sweltering-hot flat.

I then have an idea. This morning we read that Mila is now at the age where she should begin to laugh. On reading this we spent the day tickling her feet, doing silly dances, flaring our nostrils and making funny noises. Alas we haven't even managed to raise so much as a snigger. We're disappointed, but also relieved that this means that Mila probably isn't a Daily Star reader. But maybe the unusual sight of an old man in pants will make Mila giggle! I fetch our baby girl and show her the old man in pants. Mila just stares at him and frowns.

The following morning and Zsuzsa has left me alone with our sleeping cub. I'm very proud of myself as I've been ultra-productive while Mila sleeps. I've been beavering away with a work project and I've also done some rigorous exercise.

I'm about to jump in the shower when I hear something. A baby crying. Fudgenuts! I eventually decide to solve this crying-baby, stinky-body conundrum by bringing Mila's play mat into the bathroom so that I can keep an eye on her while I shower. I plonk Mila down on the floor, switch on the shower, let my dressing gown drop and I'm about to step into the steamy hot water when I hear a noise that I haven't heard before. It's a laugh. A baby laugh. My baby's laugh.

I turn to Mila to see what on earth could be so funny. What could it be? One of her cuddly toys? A strange sound? Has she just discovered her own feet? None of the above. It's Daddy's 'bits'. She has suddenly decided that Daddy's 'bits' are hilarious. Brilliant.

"Ok, Mila. You can stop your giggling now."

But Mila is having none of it. Her little baby face is contorted with hilarity. It's apparently the funniest thing that she's ever seen in all of her nine weeks on Earth.

I point my baby in the other direction, continue with my self-conscious shower and reminisce about those halcyon days before Mila learnt to laugh.

Day 126

Blame it on the Bogey

"Honey, I've read something on the internet." says my wife, before adding, "But please don't judge me."

This sounds intriguing. So much so that I immediately stop crushing candy and sit up straight.

"I'm going to put some cabbage on my nipples. But first I'm going to iron it."

I'm not sure what to say.

"Apparently it's good for breast feeding injuries."

Okay. Now it makes a little bit more sense…I guess.

"I know what you're thinking." Zsuzsa says. "You're thinking this is another crazy Hungarian remedy aren't you!? You're thinking this is another tomato-gate!"

I was actually wondering how easy it would be to iron a cabbage, but let me tell you about tomato-gate. Last year I had an ingrowing toenail. It was agony and I was struggling to walk. Zsuzsa assured me that she knew how to fix it. She then put a beef tomato on my toe and wrapped it in cling-film. I was in so much pain that I went along with it. The next morning I removed the cling-film, pulled the beef tomato off my toe and washed off all the excess tomato juice. My ingrowing toenail was still ingrowing. I decided to go old school and went to see a doctor.

"You are aren't you!? Look at you, looking down at my methods with your snobby British nose! I bet you don't even believe in aloe vera do you!?"

At this point I'd just like to mention that I haven't said a word.

"Well I'm going to iron some cabbage and stuff it down my bra, no matter what you say!"

Zsuzsa storms off.

I must confess though, beef tomato and cabbage bras aren't the only Hungarian medical practise that have surprised me since arriving in Budapest. I think I've mentioned this before, but shortly after Mila was born, she began to make breathing noises in her sleep that suggested that she smoked forty cigarettes a day. On the assumption that she wasn't an exceptionally crafty smoker, we took Mila to see a doctor. The doctor did a few checks and to our relief said everything was normal. He did however recommend that we use something called an orrszi-porszi.

"What's an orrszi-porszi? I later asked Zsuzsa.

"It's a hoover attachment for baby's noses. You attach it to your hoover and then stick it up the baby's nose. It sucks out all of the bad stuff."

"What? A real hoover?"

"Yes. A real hoover. It's good for preventing eye or ear infections"

I was sceptical, but lo and behold she was right. I've never seen these things in the UK, but apparently Hungarians swear by them and they seem to do the trick.

The first few times that we tried it on Mila she seemed surprised, but didn't actually seem to mind the whole sucking process so much. Recently however, Mila is starting to kick up a big stink whenever we stick a hoover attachment up her nose. What a princess! It's become quite a rigmarole. Annoyingly, this evening we've noticed a big bogey up Mila's nose and in the interest of a good night's sleep, we are considering rolling out the orrszi-porszi one more time.

"I think it's actually the noise of the hoover that Mila doesn't like so much." says Zsuzsa. "Maybe if we blast out really loud music right by her ears we can mask the sound of the hoover?"

"Hmmm."

"Hmmm."

"It would have to be music that we would quite like her to hate though." I add. "In case she learns to associate the tune with the nose hoover."

"Hmmm."

"Hmmm."

"What about ABBA?" Zsuzsa suggests.

Five minutes later and Mila is having her nose hoovered, her shrill baby screams being drowned out by the sound of "Dancing Queen".

That night Mila sleeps like a snot-free little log. We drift off to our sweet dreams as the melodic sounds of nocturnal Budapest dance upon our eardrums and the fragrant scent of freshly ironed cabbage wafts through the night sky.

Day 133
Planes, Trains and Bull Sherbert

Zsuzsa is on a plane. Her eyes are wide, her skin an extraordinary shade of crimson and a stream of dirty expletives are pouring from her mouth.

She's just realised that one of her breasts is hanging out for all to see. She'd been breast feeding, but it's now been about thirty minutes since nipple and baby mouth were separated.

"I thought we'd agreed not to swear around Mila?" I say as Zsuzsa tucks herself away.

"I've spent the last half hour sitting on a plane with a boob out!", responds Zsuzsa. "I even chatted to the air stewardess about the sandwiches! I think it's okay to swear!"

The no-swearing rule is in response to Mila who has begun to try and mimic what we say. And although Alistair McGowan has little to fear at this moment, we've suggested that we replace swearwords with child-friendly alternatives. The trouble is that we both have fairly filthy potty mouths, so it's not so easy.

"Now I know why the old guy in seat 8C keeps smiling at me!" Zsuzsa adds, as she tries to shrink into her seat.

Our airplane adventure is all due to the fact that my brother is getting married in deepest, darkest Wales, and we've decided that that is as good a reason as any to unleash our cub upon the British public.

So, with seemingly the entire contents of our flat as well as our twelve week old baby full of pooh (she last defecated five days ago), we made our way through security in record time, queue skipping like a Frenchman and now here we sit, on the BA flight from Budapest to London Heathrow.

"I wouldn't worry about it." says the elderly Hungarian lady sitting next to me. She's been eavesdropping on our conversation and was therefore aware of Zsuzsa's brazen display of exhibitionism. "Nobody seems to mind."

I smile at the lady, happy at her reassuring words. About ten minutes later I realise what a grave error this was as she has seemingly taken this simple mouth movement as an open invitation to use me as a soundboard for her never-ending world of pain. For the next hour the lady proceeds to unload her woes upon me. A few highlights being that she's confined to a wheelchair due to a spinal injury, has cancer in her left kidney, was deaf until the age of three, has a rare cinnamon allergy, severe diabetes and hardly ever sees her family as they all live in America. I'm about to open the plane door and end it all, when Mila comes to the rescue with her own homemade version of smelling salts. It's unmistakable and it smacks me in the nostrils. She's decided that enough is enough and proudly joined an exclusive club of two, that club consisting of people that I know who've shat their pants a mile in the air. The other member probably wouldn't appreciate me unmasking him so let's just call him Saul.

Thankfully, the rest of the flight goes without a hitch and we're very proud of our well-behaved little madam. She didn't cry, she didn't scream, she didn't make us the broken parents on a plane with the apologetic eyes. As we leave the flight the elderly Hungarian lady asks for our number and suggests we meet up in January. She also asks if she can be Mila's Godmother.

"Why don't we take your number instead?" I suggest, terror rising inside.

Our feet touch British soil and I am happy. Soon I can show my family what I've made, but first we have a long train journey to look forward to. To help with a smooth transition I've planned ahead and organised a taxi to greet us at arrivals. I scan the crowd of waiting taxi drivers for my name. Nothing. I decide not to panic. I'm sure they're here somewhere. I call the taxi rank. They're twenty minutes away. I try to stay calm. Twenty minutes go by and still no taxi. I call them. The driver has gone to the wrong terminal.

"SON OF A BIN MAN!"

I give him a call. He hangs up on me.

"WHAT AN UTTER BAR STOOL!"

I call HQ. They arrange another driver. He'll be with us in thirty minutes.

"THIRTY MINUTES! THIRTY FUDGING MINUTES! THIS IS BULL SHERBERT!"

I make a mental note never to use this massive bunch of cockerels again.

Day 140
Hallelujah!

"My mother wants to ask you something." says Zsuzsa.

"Really? What does she want to ask me?" I reply.

"Well, she was wondering if you'd mind singing Hallelujah at this year's Christmas Advent gathering."

"…"

"I mean you wouldn't be singing alone, you'd have lots of children as backing singers."

"…"

"It would be to the entire village."

"…"

"Honey, are you alright? You've gone a bit pale."

"…"

Several minutes pass.

"I'm sorry. What?" I eventually respond.

"Sing Hallelujah to the entire village backed up by a bunch of children."

At this point I'd like to mention that I am not a professional singer. I'm not even an amateur singer. I vaguely remember once singing a karaoke rendition of a live song at University after drinking several Aftershocks, but that was the current highlight of my singing career.

Wait a Goddamn second! What the devil ever happened to Aftershock (the potent, cinnamon-flavoured, highly alcoholic spirit)? Is it hanging out in a retirement home somewhere with Mighty White Bread and Blockbuster Video?

"But…why me?" I say, utterly befuddled.

"Mum thinks it would be nice to have someone sing in a different language to Hungarian, plus she's heard you singing in the shower and thinks you have a nice voice."

I ponder this for a moment. Maybe I shouldn't simply dismiss this in a blink of an eye. Maybe this is what life is all about? Maybe it's all about challenging yourself, living life and pushing the boundaries? Maybe it's all about singing to the entire inhabitants of a remote Hungarian village whilst supported by a bunch of children. Hang on! Heard me singing in the shower! Surely all showers are soundproof!?

"Why don't you find the song on YouTube and sing along to it?" Zsuzsa suggests.

Spurred on by a sudden desire to grab life by the testicles, I search YouTube and find the Jeff Buckley version. I get the lyrics in front of me and nervously begin to sing the song to my expectant audience of wife and baby daughter. Five seconds later and Zsuzsa, channelling Simon Cowell, puts her hand up to stop me. Surely I wasn't that bad?

"Not that one." she says.

She obviously means the Leonard Cohen original.

"The Alexandra Burke version!"

"Alexandra Burke!? Alexandra Burke the winner of the 2008 series of The X Factor!? No fudging way!"

I decide that not only do I know a little too much about Alexandra Burke, but also that life is probably not all about singing Alexandra Burke songs to Hungarian villagers.

Day 144
Déjà Pooh

"Honey! Can you please stop watching the election!? Mila keeps looking at the light on your phone and won't go to sleep!" Zsuzsa whispers loudly.

"But it's the American election! A historic moment! I just want to watch it until some of the results come in so that I can sleep soundly knowing that The Donald isn't going to win."

I'm actually watching an iguana fight a gang of snakes on YouTube.

"Okay, but at least go under the covers or something so that Mila can't see the light."

Under the covers I go. Things are not looking good for the iguana.

I *have* been watching the election. The reptilian battle-royal was just a brief respite from the political, potential catastrophe. For the last couple of days I've had a horrible feeling that the orange, leather faced, sex-pesty one was going to clinch it. The polls and the bookies all suggested that Hilary was going to reign victorious, but we've been here before haven't we? My impending doom-sensors had been tingling. Less than five months ago I lay in the same bed in our Budapest flat, heavily pregnant wife beside me and watched in horror as my home country slowly committed hari kari and voted to leave the

EU. Now, I'm lying here again, 20% poorer due to the bastardly Brexit, wife and three month old baby by my side, worrying about the state of the world in which little Mila will blossom.

"Run you crazy little iguana! Run as fast as your scaly little legs will carry you! You must escape the clutches of these slithery beasts!"

It's been a funny day full of anniversaries and achievements. It's exactly a year ago since my first book, Ferocious Dennis was published, and also exactly a year ago since Mila became more than just a twinkle in her mother's eye. I've also started a new job at a funky media agency in the beating heart of Pest. I should be happy and proud, but there is an ominous orange shadow hanging over me, breathing its foreboding breath upon the nape of my neck.

A few minutes later and I'm still under the covers clutching my phone. Things are not looking good. The iguana is hopelessly outnumbered as the dastardly snakes attack! As well as that, the first results from the first few states have trickled through. Trump is leading 19 to 3. I quickly check The New York Times forecaster. They are still predicting a Clinton victory with an 82% likelihood. Good odds, but I'm still uneasy. Maybe it's the sense of déjà vu engulfing me.

"Honey! Mila can still see the light through the duvet! Please! I need to get to sleep and you've got work in the morning."

"Okay, okay."

"How's it looking?"

"Well Trump is ahead, but the forecasts are still predicting a

Clinton win. Maybe he was always predicted to win these states."

I don't know who I'm trying to convince. Zsuzsa or myself. If it's myself I'm doing a lousy job.

I watch the iguana make a miraculous escape, decide enough is enough, put my phone down and try to go to sleep. It takes a while, but I eventually drift off. I dream that I am in Wales. I'm in my recently deceased Grandma's house. Donald Trump is sitting in her chair. He's wearing an ill-fitting t-shirt with a Welsh flag design. He's just sitting there, staring at me with his stupid face and silly hair flapping about. A snake slithers passed. I hear a baby cooing and I'm yanked from my dreamland. It's Mila. She's decided that as its 06:00, it's time to wake up. I reach for my phone, check the news. Bum. This is like Steve Brookstein winning The X-Factor all over again, but much, much worse.

A few hours later and I'm in the office for my second day at work. I'm sitting on the toilet reading the outpouring of woe on social media. I reach for the toilet paper. Holy mother of God! There isn't any! Armageddon has already begun! I sit there panicking for a few moments trying to work out what to do? What would Batman do if he was stuck on a toilet, on his second day at a new workplace? I decide that he'd probably keep some spare toilet paper in his utility belt, the uber-prepared rubber-suited prick! Well screw you and your utility belt Batman! I'm going to do this my way! So, absolutely terrified, I stealthily make my way across the toilet room floor, shuffling like a penguin with my trousers around my ankles. I successfully complete my mission. I will be clean! I will not have an unspeakable second day at work that will haunt me forever!

Back at my desk I ponder the events of the last 24 hours or so. Things are looking decidedly bleak, but then I remember our friend the iguana. Things didn't look great for the iguana, but did he give up? Did he fuck!

Maybe that's the answer! Maybe we should all be more iguana. Either way, I'm sure things will be alright in the end.

They will won't they?

The most thrilling action sequence of all time?

Day 153

Don't Go into The Water

I'm sitting alone by the side of a swimming pool, bone dry except for the pair of urine drenched swimming trunks that I'm currently sporting. I'm watching a group of Hungarian ladies teach their babies to swim. I feel like a raging weirdo. I look like a raging weirdo! How did I get here? Well it began a few days ago…

We're at home. Zsuzsa is on the phone whilst simultaneously changing Mila's nappy. How can she do two things at once I hear at least half of you cry? Well, I've no idea. Black magic? But anyway, she's trying to book swimming lessons for Mila, but nobody appears to be answering. Zsuzsa sighs.

"Honey." she says. "Can you watch Mila?"

BEEP!

"I'm desperate for a number two." she adds.

Her face goes whiter than a Scotsman's torso on the first day of a beach holiday.

"What's up?" I ask.

"The answering machine! I think I've just told the swimming instructor that I'm desperate for a number two!"

"Ha!"

"What are we going to do!? I can't face her now!"

"Why, because she'll know that you're one of those people who sometimes needs a number two?"

"No! Because she'll think I'm one of those people who rings people up to tell them that they need a number two!"

It's a few days later. We arrive at the swimming pool. Zsuzsa has begged me to be the one who takes Mila into the pool, just so that she doesn't have to face the lady who knows what she gets up to when she's all alone. After much protestation I agree, when Zsuzsa reassures me that most of the class will be men and it'll be in English.

I enter the swimming pool area. It's my turn to resemble a Scotsman's torso. There's not a Y chromosome in sight. I mean some of the babies might be boys, but let's be honest, who knows? They all look like Ross Kemp at this age. Not ideal, but I can get through this. The instructor approaches me. She speaks to me in Hungarian at one hundred miles per hour.

"Uh...Beszél Angolul? (Uh...Do you speak English?) I respond.

"Nem." (No)

"Oh." (Oh)

All eyes in the room then turn and look at me. Like a pack of wolves they can sense weakness. I take a deep breath, pull myself together and find a changing table. I change Mila into her swimming nappy, pick her up and put her on my knee. We watch together as the ladies in the pool begin singing Hungarian nursery rhymes to their babies. That's right! Hungarian nursery rhymes! It's official. I am in hell.

I whisper in Mila's ear. "This is horrific."

My little baby looks up at me and smiles. My heart melts and I feel a warm sensation. It's baby piss. My shorts are drenched in baby piss.

Out of the blue and unexpectedly a swimming-costume-clad Zsuzsa appears.

"Honey! It's okay Honey. I'm going to do this."

Before I can say a word she grabs Mila and they both join the group of Hungarian women. Actually what's the collective for a group of Hungarian women? A goulash maybe?

And so we're now back at the beginning. Back with me looking like a raging weirdo, alone and naked except for my urine drenched shorts. I spot my escape route. A sauna. With my hands covering my baby piss trunks I make my way to the sauna and plonk myself down in a dark corner. Forty five minutes later, when the coast is clear, I re-emerge. I'm hotter than the sun. I've never liked swimming lessons.

Day 160

The Number 2

I'm in our car with my little, oestrogen-infused family, hurtling towards Zsuzsa's parents' house, which is nestled in a little village near Eger. I'm smiling at myself in the mirror. Out of the corner of my beady eyes I notice Zsuzsa watching me. She looks perplexed.

"What are you doing?" she asks.

"Practicing my smile." I reply. "I'm thinking about developing a new one."

"Why?"

"Well I'm just not sure it's a perfect smile for the camera. I think I can do better."

I continue to work on my new smile.

"Maybe I should get my teeth whitened." I add.

"You don't need your teeth whitened honey"

"Um, I think you're forgetting that I'm a TV presenter now. I don't want them looking all murky on screen."

Zsuzsa sighs. "You're not a TV presenter."

I decide to ignore this cruel comment as I have work to do. I have a new smile to craft.

My tooth related conundrum is due to the fact that I've recently signed a contract with The Dad Network to be a vlogger for them. This means that I'll be making videos for baby-related products as well as creating videos for Warner Bros who The Dad Network are in partnership with. Earlier in the week I received my first brief. Create a 2-3 minute video with the title "How to Change a Nappy".

I've spent the last few days filming and crafting my magnum opus. It's called 'The Number 2' and it's my 'Citizen Kane' of instructional YouTube clips. My 'Lawrence of Arabia' of shitty nappy films. It's 3 minutes long and it's unquestonably a nappy-changing video of epic scale. It has drama, twists and humour, and undoubted chemistry between the two movie leads, Gareth Michael Hutchins and Mila Juno Hutchins. The surprise cameo from Zsuzsa Ferencz is also a high point, and hotly tipped to take home the Oscar for best cameo in an instructional YouTube clip for Dads. Feeling very much like Martin Scorsese, I send my masterpiece off to The Dad Network for review.

A few days later and I get a reply. It's great news!

"So Warner Bros LOVE you and want you to do the official How to videos! Warners showed it to an 18 to 25-year-old audience who thought it was excellent!" the email reads.

Woo hoo!

"They love it honey!" I bellow to Zsuzsa who is no doubt somewhere in the flat, tit out with a baby attached to her nipple.

"Hooray!" comes a distant reply.

I then sit down to watch the Warner Bros edit that they've also sent to me. Hmmm. That's weird. What's this music? Uh...they appear to have omitted my "WHY HAST THOU FORSAKEN ME!" speech. The fools! That was a really powerful bit with real gravitas! I carry on watching. What!? Where's my joke about Tupperware parties! That joke was comedy gold! I shrug off the Tupperware blow and continue to watch the edit. Whoah! Whoah! Whoah! My Rocky speech! Where's my Rocky speech!? You can't have a video on how to change a baby's nappy without a Rocky Balboa speech!

The video ends. I sit there, motionless. Zsuzsa appears.

"What's wrong honey?" she asks.

"My film. That's not my original vision." I say.

"Don't worry honey. It's still great and at least you're getting paid. You're a professional film maker now!"

I consider her words and decide that she's probably right. This is probably a common occurrence for filmmakers. I'm just another director battling a film studio. People will just have to wait for the Blu-ray release of my director's cut edition of 'How to Change a Nappy' to see my original vision.

I pull myself together, go online and order some tooth whitening gel.

Day 167

The Foreign Grocery Zone

On request from my wife I'm in a Spar in Budapest searching for rice milk. She's read somewhere that it's great for breastfeeding Mums.

"Plus Mila really likes it", she adds.

Our four-month-old baby might still be getting to grips with her bodily functions, but she's a woman who knows what she wants, and that's rice milk.

My quest, you may think, is simple enough, but you, sir/madam, are naive. I'm sorry to break this to you, but you are. For this place is a jungle of Zs, És and the eternally baffling Ös. It's like The Crystal Maze if The Crystal Maze had a foreign grocery zone. I've been wandering up and down this forest of similar, but not quite familiar food items for what seems like days now and I'm flummoxed. I can't find it in the refrigerated section, I can't find it with the soya milk.

"Where art thou rice milk!"

I've been racking my brains without success. What on Earth is the Hungarian for rice milk? Usually on occasions like this I would turn to my trusty companion, my Man Friday, my Dr Watson, my Ant or Dec. I'm of course referring to my translation app on my phone, but as luck would have it, the Spar near my home in Budapest is isolated from the rest of the Earth. All around it, perfect signal. Step through the Spar doors, it's 1995.

I eventually decide that enough is enough and locate an elderly member of staff to help me.

"Beszel Angolul? (Do You speak English)" I ask hopefully.

"A little" he replies.

"I'm looking for the rice milk?" I say, instantly wondering why I've made that a question.

The old man stares at me blankly. It would appear that his little English doesn't include 'rice milk'. But its okay. No need to panic. I know exactly what to do. I've got this.

"Riiiiiice meeeeeelk?" I ask hopefully, now sounding like Dracula.

"Ah!" the man says, and directs me to follow him.

And off we go, slowly wending our merry way through the Spar, my guide leading me, skilfully navigating through the aisles one by one. I'm full of gratitude as a part of me was beginning to wonder if this was it. If I was to spend eternity in this place, forever searching for an unsweetened milk substitute derived from brown rice. I study him as he slowly trudges through the store. I think to myself how nice of the Spar to employ someone of his age. They should be commended! He must be at least 75, and not that easy on his feet any more. Bravo Spar!

And then it hits me.

HE DOESN'T WORK HERE! Oh dear Lord! I've accosted a random elderly gent wearing a red top and convinced him to help me find rice milk. It's now also beginning to dawn on me that he doesn't actually seem to know where the rice milk is! He's led us to the confectionary aisle and is currently scouring it at a snail's pace! Who is this mad man!?

I'm beginning to panic. We are now two men who don't speak a common language, inexplicably tied to one another until we find the elusive rice milk. My palms are getting clammy. I need to do something.

"It's okay." I say. "I'll find the rice milk on my own."

The man simply smiles back at me and then gestures for me to follow. He has no idea what I'm talking about. What on Earth is the Hungarian for "It's okay. I'll find the rice milk on my own."

About twenty minutes later and I breathe a huge sigh of relief as we accidentally stumble across the rice milk (bizarrely by the tinned peaches). I express my gratitude to the old man by saying "thank you" but with Dracula's accent, head to the check-out and leave the shop as quickly as my little legs will carry me. I arrive home and hand my wife the rice milk. Go for your life, mammary glands!

"Why have you bought rice pudding?" says Zsuzsa.

Damn you random old man wearing red in the Spar.

Day 174
National Lampoon's Prague Vacation

Zsuzsa and I have been locked in a tumultuous tussle about Christmas trees. I want a massive tree smothered in lights and shiny things, whereas Zsuzsa want a tiny tree that can sit on our dining table (Grinch!).

I'm now driving my family to Prague. About an hour into the drive it hits me. I'm Chevy Chase! I'm the man with a family who wants to have the biggest tree in the world, a house covered in fairy-lights and who also gets overly excited about the prospect of family road trips! Oh my God! Have I always been Chevy Chase and just not realised it, or is it something that's happened very recently, since fatherhood happened? I mean, I do love Chevy Chase and think both National Lampoon's Vacation and National Lampoon's European Vacation are things of rare beauty, but the realisation still hits me pretty hard.

About two hours later, we're in Slovakia and need to stop at a service station to change Mila's nappy. Zsuzsa wanders off to find a changing area while I attempt to buy a coffee from the most serious, gruff looking Slovak that has ever lived. The man stares at me with his sad, Slovakian face. He seems to be a broken man with cartoon stubble and soulless, dead eyes. A moment goes by and I suddenly realise that I have been trying to make him smile. I have been using the same tried and tested technique that I use on Mila. It consists of me making eye contact with Mila and then repeatedly smiling an exaggerated smile at Mila like a lunatic. With Mila, this works nearly every time. She loves it. The Slovak service station attendant though, apparently doesn't love it. He just glares at me. I decide to stop trying to make him smile.

"Do you speak English?" I ask. "No!" he responds.

This throws me a bit as his answer suggests that he might do, but he doesn't seem to be the joking kind so I try another option.

"Magyar beszél (Do you speak Hungarian)?" "Nem! (No!)"

Again I'm confused by his answer, but I decide to let it pass. It's time to resort to technology. I whip out my app (that's not a euphemism), and type in the Slovak for coffee. I show it to him. Take that Slovak service station man (which incidentally sounds like an awful super hero film)!

After a stunted conversation in which the man told me that all they serve is espresso, I ordered an espresso and he then gave me a cappuccino, I return to the dining area. The only place available to change Mila is a bench in the middle of the room. Zsuzsa is well into the changing process. Mila has her nappy off, naked little legs, baby butt and baby bits in the air. She seems to be having the time of her life and she's smiling wildly at all of the miserable looking Slovakian truck drivers munching their way through equally miserable looking sandwiches.

"I hope she grows out of this." I say to Zsuzsa. "It would be unfortunate to get a phone call in twenty years' time, telling us that Mila is half naked in the dining area of a Slovakian service station, smiling at truck drivers."

About two hours later and we are now in the Czech Republic. We are approaching a city named Brno. Mila is letting out little baby snores from the back of the car and I'm doing my best to make sense of a fairly treacherous-looking road.

"Honey." says Zsuzsa. "Did you know that this week, last weekend, was the first week, last year of my first trimester?"

It's fair to say that I did not know this, largely due to the fact that I have no idea what that sentence means.

"What?" I reply.

"This week, last weekend" she repeats. "It was the first week, last year, of my first trimester."

It's too late. After five hours of driving this sentence is the straw that broke the camel's back. I've accidentally turned off the motorway and we are now heading into the heart of Brno.

"Where are we going?" Zsuzsa asks.

"I don't know!" I respond. "You twisted my mind with your crazy sentence and I lost my concentration!"

I check the sat nav. Okay. No major issue. There's a roundabout coming up, we can just go all the way around the roundabout and get back on track. We enter the roundabout.

"Did you understand what I was saying?" Zsuzsa asks. "About

my first trimester?"

Aaaarrrghhh! She's done it again. I accidentally thought about the sentence again, she's bamboozled me and I've missed the turn! We are going round and round in circles on a roundabout in the middle of a random Czech city that seems to have lost some of its vowels. It's like that scene in European Vacation when they drive round and round the roundabout in London.

"Look kids! Houses of parliament! Big Ben!"

I am Chevy Chase.

Day 181

The Hair Atrocity

"Can you come with me to the hairdressers to tell them what I want?" I ask Zsuzsa.

"You don't need me to come. You can speak enough Hungarian to let them know." she replies.

But then I remember the last time I went to a Hungarian hairdressers, when they cut my hair a little too short.

"I'm not sure." I say.

"Honey, just ask for a little haircut."

"What if they try and make me look Hungarian? What if I come out with a moustache?"

"You'll be fine."

Thirty minutes later and I'm venturing into the local hairdressers. I'm alone and scared, but this shaggy hair isn't going to cut itself. I approach the scissor-wielding staff and ask the dreaded question.

"Beszél Angolul (Do you speak English?)?"

"Errrr, nem."

Son of a bin man! I take a moment to compose myself. I

convince myself that all is okay. I speak a little Hungarian. I know how to ask for 'A little hair cut'. I've got this! I take a deep breath, ask for, what I later realise is "A little hair" and take my place in the judgement seat. The hairdresser today is a trendy gent. He's clad from head to toe in black, with skinny jeans, a tight fitting t-shirt and a black beanie hat. He seems confident in what he has to do. And so it begins.

The first ten minutes of the haircut are incident free. He sprays a little water, trims a little hair and circles me repeatedly like a prowling tiger.

We enter the second half of the haircut and it's now that proceedings will take an unexpected twist. The hairdresser, who I think I'll call Laszlo, whips out a big canister of hair mousse and a hairdryer. He then begins to build my hair up, and up, and up, slathering on dollop after dollop of mousse and using the hairdryer as a weapon of mass volumisation. All I can do is sit and watch in bewildered horror, unable to communicate with my hair aggressor. It's like watching a car crash happen in slow motion, but with more hair and a lot more hair mousse.

The hair cut finishes with a little hair spray. I mean, of course it does! I stare at my reflection. WHAT THE HOLY FUCK DID I ASK FOR!? I look insane! I look like a hipster from the 80's! I look like a mixture of Jedward, Eraserhead and Joan Collins! I look like a sodding cockatoo!

"Okay?" asks Laszlo.

"Igen. Köszönöm. (Yes. Thanks)" I reply and give him a tip.

After all, I'm British.

I leave the hairdresser, stooping low to navigate my hair through the doorway, and stand in the crisp, Hungarian winter's air, now a significantly taller man than I was thirty minutes ago. I wait for Zsuzsa, comforted by the knowledge that she has my hat with her. Ten minutes go by. Zsuzsa approaches. Her eyes widen.

"OH MY GOD! WHAT THE FUCK HAS HE DONE TO YOUR HEAD!?" asks Zsuzsa.

"Hat please." I reply.

This hat is staying on my head until February.

Day 188

Christmas Day

"So this is Christmas. And what have you done?"

Well, we've actually done a fair bit if you must know Mr Lennon. I've quit my job, turned 40, rented out our flat, written a film script, we've moved to Budapest and become parents for the first time to a beautiful little cub. So, all in all, a fairly eventful, epic year. And as I sit here in a remote Hungarian village surrounded by people muttering in tongues, with a belly full of what I think was goose (although I'm not entirely sure), with Home Alone playing in Hungarian in the background, I can't help but feel reflective.

One of the things that I'm reflecting on, naturally, is fatherhood. It's a fairly life changing thing that I'm still trying to fully get my melon head around. They say that you need to spend 10,000 hours doing something to become an expert at something. Well I've now been a Dad for 3,424 hours so I'm more than a third of the way to becoming a guru (my graduation date is August 25, 2017). I still have a fair amount to learn, but I'm getting there. I've at the very least progressed to intermediate level. With this in mind, seeing as it's Christmas, I thought I'd share some of the things that I've learnt in those 3,424 hours with the world…

1. Child birth is like the opening 20 minutes of Saving PrivateRyan, but for hours.

People often quote the day that their child was born as their happiest-ever day. What they usually fail to mention is that it's also one of the most terrifying, savage, brutal and tiring days of your life. At least it was for us! A lot of it was, in my imagination at least, like living through the D-Day landings. Scenes of horror with people running around, barking orders in a foreign language. Obviously there were huge moments of unadulterated joy and emotion that I'd never previously experienced, but there were also moments that still haunt me. Witnessing a baby's head doing unimaginable things to my beloved wife being one of those moments. Shudder. Apparently this isn't the case for everyone, with some women slipping the baby out as easily as shelling peas. Lucky buggers!

2. Changing a nappy is very much like mackerel fishing

You wait ages for one to come along and then you get a whole shoal of shits all at once. Plus no matter how much you scrub, no matter how much cream you apply, the scent lingers. It reminds me of my mackerel fishing adventures as a child in Tenby. I used to spend hours scrubbing my hands, smothering myself in industrial strength soap. Made no difference. I still stunk of mackerel for days.

3. Cleaning up shit is never joyous.

Staying with nappies for a moment, one of the most daunting prospects of parenthood for me was having to clean up shit. I mean, I've never liked cleaning up other people's shit. People said, "You won't mind when it's your own." Well you know what? Bullshit! Changing a shitty nappy is, and always will be, a chore. I might prefer to clean up my babies shit than clean up your shit for example (no offence), but when you open that nappy and see fresh jalfrezi staring back up at you, your heart will always weep. I also had a 'moment', about three weeks into fatherhood, when a friend with a two-year-old kid informed me that this nappy changing malarkey goes on for at least a couple of years! I almost passed out.

4. Your evenings are screwed for the next fifteen odd years.

A similar moment of clarity hit me a few days ago. Our little human cub is now 20 weeks old. Naturally we put her to bed each evening and the whole process is often quite a rigmarole (she, like many of us, doesn't want to sleep before getting a mouth full of titty). I don't know why it hadn't occurred to me before, but I suddenly realised that we're going to have to do this for more than a decade! Christ on a Segway!

5. Grandparents are worth their weight in gold. Even the fat ones.

Given point 4, the one thing that keeps me sane is knowing that we have some grandparents around to help out and let us pretend to be the humans that we once were every now and then. Initially I was concerned that I'd find the help from the in-laws overbearing. Now, whenever there's a knock on the door and their smiling, Hungarian faces enter I shed a solitary tear of euphoric joy. Finally someone to hand my baby to, so that I can take a five minute break! The first time that they baby-sat and we escaped to the cinema to watch Bridget Jones 3 with subtitles, has probably made it into the top 5 of my 'life's greatest moments'.

6. I can't make up my Goddamn mind!

Whenever Mila is asleep I want to wake her up. Whenever Mila is awake I want her to go to sleep. What's that about?

7. Having a baby is like the Blitz.

Six months ago I would have struggled to comprehend how we could function on close to no sleep, smothered in shit, confined to our flat and with something small and fleshy screaming in our ear for hours on end. Now I know we can manage because we have to. We also often find ourselves running to our bunker when we suspect that our exploding baby bomb is about to go off.

Basically, we keep calm and carry on.

8. Babies are wind machines.

Mila has a few hobbies, but one of her clear favourites is breaking wind. She's a beast! Sleeping in the same room as her is like sleeping with a darts player after curry night at Weatherspoon. How can all of this come from something so small and sweet!?

9. Babies breathe like a middle-aged white man dances.

Nobody told me this beforehand, but babies stop breathing for just long enough for you to think that they're fucking dead, before they start breathing again. It's like a middle-aged white man dancing at a wedding. It has no rhythm and is not cool. The number of times I've checked on Mila and gone cold when she doesn't seem to be breathing, only for her to then let our one big breath. What is this sadistic madness!?

10. It's amazing.

It's tough, it's emotional, we bicker, we cry, we would chop off our own genitals for a lie in, but it's genuinely incredible. You may have had a tough night, but when you wake up and look at your baby, and see a beautiful little face smiling back at you, it's a thing of pure joy. It's indescribable (despite my best efforts to describe it). Being there to experience Mila grow and develop on a daily basis is priceless, and the risky, some would say bat-shit-mental, decisions that we took earlier this year have turned out to be inspired. Being a parent is wonderful and awe-inspiring and despite the nappy changing, the lack of sleep and the logistical nightmare that our life has become, we wouldn't have it any other way.

Day 194

The Spa Break

It's Boxing Day and we are driving to a spa hotel in a place in Hungary called Heviz. I'm finding something that Zsuzsa has just told me difficult to compute.

"The hotel has its own free dental service?" I ask with furrowed brow.

"Yes." replies Zsuzsa, as though it's the most normal thing in the world.

"That's really weird."

"Why is it weird?"

"Because it's a hotel with a free dental service! I've heard of hotels that have free bikes for you to use, but never one that has free dentists for you to use."

"Maybe they saw a gap in the market?"

"But that's mental! What's next? A double room with a free continental breakfast and a colonic irrigation?"

A few hours later and we have arrived at the hotel, and despite the dental insanity everything seems normal. In fact the place seems lovely! Zsuzsa, Mila and I are relaxing by the pool. Mila is beyond fascinated by the place. She is scanning the room with an expression of wide-eyed wonder, but this isn't surprising seeing as she has a similar expression when she rediscovers her feet every morning. Zsuzsa spots a sign that apparently says that there will be a Russian sauna session tomorrow.

"You should go honey." she says.

"What's a Russian sauna session?"

"I'm not sure. They probably put vodka on the coals or something."

It's now tomorrow and I'm lined up outside a sauna waiting for the sauna instructor to arrive. People are starting to gather and I'm beginning to wonder why they are all wrapped in white cotton sheets. The sauna instructor arrives carrying an ice box and people begin to enter. I hand my ticket to the instructor.

"Nem szabad (not allowed)." says the instructor, pointing to my shorts.

It now dawns on me. Everyone around me, both men and women, are naked under their sheets. Some of the more brazen people are already actually dropping their sheets, revealing their unmentionables, and let me tell you, these are not pretty unmentionables. They have no right to be so brazen. I can only assume that they work in fairgrounds and have only ever seen themselves naked in a hall of mirrors. I hesitate. What should I do? But then I figure 'when in Heviz' and sheepishly attempt to remove my shorts under a sheet, almost falling on my face in the process.

Three minutes later and I'm in the sauna, having taken my seat on the second rung of benches. Fat, sweaty, hairy, naked Russians are all around me, as far as the eye can see. This is not how things looked in the brochure. A flabby, hairy man in his late fifties enters. He's wearing a sheet, but it's too high up, not leaving anything to the imagination. He scans the room for a space to plonk his naked, fuzzy arse. The only space is behind me so he begins clambering over bodies. He reaches me and lifts one leg over my shoulder, straddling me to get a foot hold on the rung above me. And then it happened.

About eight years ago I was in a car crash on the M25. Thankfully nobody was injured, but it was a fairly scary moment. I vividly remember seeing a lorry approaching the side of our car via my peripheral vision. I remember time slowing down and my brain working overtime to assess the situation. I remember feeling strangely calm as I accepted that an impact was inevitable, but that we'd probably be alright. I also remember thinking that I needed to keep facing forward as that was the best option to avoid serious injury.

Memories of this car crash came flooding back as I sat there in the sauna. From my peripheral vision I could see it coming my way. A saggy scrotum swinging like a pendulum. It was swinging towards the side of my face with surprising velocity. Time slowed down and I was both horrified and yet serene as I waited for the inevitable. I knew if I jerked my head too suddenly in another direction I could come to rest between an obese gent's nether regions and I was also certain that I didn't want to turn towards this atrocity and take this scrotal impact head on. And so I waited, motionless as the sweaty ball bag smacked into the side of my precious face. SPLAT! And then I just sat there, stunned and horrified as the sauna session began. Vodka was poured on the coals. Russian music began blaring, a Russian flag was used to waft the heat around the room. The heat was excruciating and yet my mind was elsewhere. I was fantasising about dipping my face into a vat of white spirits and then scrubbing my face clean off, but I had thirty minutes to endure beforehand.

Thirty minutes later and I bolt out of the sauna. I'm hotter than the sun. I throw my swimming trunks on and clamber into the plunge pool. I cool down and then begin my ascent up the ladder, out of the ice water. I look up and then I see it.

My ball-bag aggressor, completely naked, climbing down the ladder towards me. BACKWARDS! I have now seen every millimetre of this man. I have seen true horror.

I move with pace and purpose, past my wife, towards the shower.

"How was the sauna honey? Honey? What's wrong? Honey? Honey?"

Boldog Új Évet (Happy New Year).

Day 201

The Bad Arse

We're in a coffee shop near our home. It's a lovely little coffee shop with a 1920's New York style interior and jazz music playing in the background. If Woody Allen was not an American-Jewish actor/writer/director, but instead a coffee shop based in Budapest, he'd be this coffee shop. Mila is lounging by the window, relaxing after a strenuous morning of nappy changing while Zsuzsa and I are chatting about my film script whilst waiting for our drinks to arrive.

"It's a bit like that film." says Zsuzsa.

"Which film?" I ask.

"The one with the man in. You know? The man with the brown hair."

I nod in agreement. As I'm sure you are all aware, now that she's narrowed it down to every film ever made except for Finding Nemo, Zsuzsa must be referring to the Hollywood remake of Oldboy starring the brown haired actor, Josh Brolin. But if I'm honest, I'm not really paying that much attention as I have something else on my mind. One of my New Year's resolutions this year is to force myself to speak Hungarian. I mean, it seems like the sensible thing to do if I have any desire to minimise situations where I'm ordering Irish coffees at 9am or being smacked in the face by a Russian man's testicles. Spurred on by this mission I've been muddling through conversations since 00:01

on January 1st. Some conversations are proving easier than others. For example I've just ordered a coffee for myself and a fruit tea infusion for my lovely wife. It was a doddle, but it hasn't all been plain sailing. Take yesterday for example…

I'm in an office that I frequent a couple of days a week. I'm on my way back to my desk from the kitchen, when I spot a lady who usually sits near me. She's standing at a chest high desk, typing away on her laptop. I've seen such things before. People with bad backs do this. With my New Year's resolution in mind I decide to converse with the lady in her native tongue. I will dazzle her with my vocabulary and ask her if she has a bad back! She will love this!

"Rossz hátsó oldal?" I say, beaming smile upon my face.

But the lady just stares at me. She looks a bit shocked. Did I get that right? Or should it have been…?

"Uh, rossz segg?"

No. That didn't seem to help. The shocked look is still there and now it's tinged with sadness. I also now realise that everyone in the office is silent and staring at us. If my office had a piano player he would have stopped playing. Slowly, and very uncomfortably, the standing lady points to her bottom with a questioning look.

"Uh" I say, smiling whilst backing away towards my desk.

I sit down and turn to the guy sitting next to me.

"What did I say?" I ask.

He leans in.

"You told her she has a bad arse." he whispers.

We're now back at the coffee shop. Zsuzsa looks at me, deep in thought.

"You're still thinking about telling that lady that she had a bad arse aren't you?" she asks.

I nod.

"Don't worry honey. You'll get there. Just keep on practicing Hungarian and you'll soon be able to speak to people without deeply insulting them."

I pick up Mila to stop her licking the window and smile meekly at my wife's kind words. A moment later and our drinks arrive. We stare at our order of coffee and fruit tea infusion in unison. They are both a nuclear yellow colour and covered in whipped cream. They also appear to be lacking in coffee, or indeed, fruit tea infusion.

"What the hell did you order honey?" ask Zsuzsa whilst sniffing her drink.

"I've no idea." I respond, whilst wondering if it's too late to swap my speaking Hungarian resolution for something less dangerous. Maybe I'll become a cage fighter instead.

Day 208

Alone in a Chateau

We're at Chateau Bela, a massive chateau in Slovakia. It's a beautiful, grandiose building with fifty spacious bedrooms/suites, a restaurant, an orangery, a spa, a bar, a private cinema, a swimming pool, a vineyard, an enormous garden and its own forest. We are the only people here. Well us, the manager, a waiter and a chef. We're also in the midst of a snow blizzard and as a result I've been keeping my beady eyes out for creepy twin girls standing at the end of every corridor.

We've just been for a candlelit meal for two (and a baby), and now we're back in the bedroom listening to the La La Land soundtrack, while I gleefully dance around our ample room in my underpants. The album has been playing on repeat on my iPhone for the best part of a week. Now, if you know me well, alarm bells may be ringing. Gareth listening to a musical soundtrack on repeat? But the man despises musicals unless they feature muppets!? Who are you and what the devil have you done with our precious Gareth? Well my friends, this is really Gareth, and the musical listening is one of the symptoms of a virus that I've recently contracted called Fatherhood. For ever since that little madam tore her way out of my beloved wife in a manner that will haunt me forever, I've been reacting differently to certain aspects of the world. Not in monumental ways, but in little ways that I look back on after they've happened and think, "Huh!".

Let's examine some of the evidence...

- I watched the film Arrival at a cinema and my eyes sprang a leak. For decades they've been impeccably well-sealed.
- I suggested that we go and see a musical (La La Land).
- We watched La La Land. I loved it. My eyes very nearly started leaking again even though I thought I'd resealed them, and I've been playing the soundtrack on repeat ever since.
- I've become increasingly intolerant of anyone intolerant (Tories, Daily Mail, The Donald, Katie Hopkins I'm looking at you).
- I was compelled to give a 1,000 forint note to a homeless man with a frozen beard (worth pointing out to non-Hungarians that that's actually only just under £3, so I haven't gone completely mental).
- I often find myself browsing the little girls clothes sections in shops and gasping at how utterly delightful a pretty little blouse is.

There are plenty more examples, but I think you should now get the picture. Basically I've become a soft bastard. Becoming a father has melted my icy heart and also made me more determined than ever to ensure that my little cub grows up in a wonderful, tolerant, open, friendly world. Plus it's made me like musicals and coo at tiny, floral dresses.

The Lads - "You fancy coming down the local and getting shit faced and then hitting a club until four in the farking morning?"

Me - "Could do. Or...how about everyone comes over to mine, we watch Dreamgirls and drink prosecco? Lads? Lads? Where are you going?"

Everyone - "Yeah we get it. You've gone soft. But to be honest we only visit your blog to read about you being an idiot and getting yourself into some kind of ridiculous situation. To be honest, we're a little disappointed"

Okay. Fair enough.

So on Wednesday I flew to London for a meeting. A guy from the office was driving to Budapest airport and he kindly agreed to pick me up and take me with him. It's 05:59 in the morning. It's dark, the temperature is sub-zero and I could easily cut glass with my tiny, rock-hard nipples. I'm standing at an agreed meeting point, a street corner about ten minutes' walk from my flat and opposite the hairdressers that did sacrilegious things to my hair. I see a car approaching. It begins to slow and pulls up about five metres away from me.

"That'll be Simon." I think to myself and jog over to the car.

I open the car door, and eager to escape the clutches of Jack Frost, I jump in. I turn and smile at Simon. But Simon doesn't smile back. As we all know, it takes Simon a while to warm up in the mornings so the fact that he doesn't respond to my smile with a smile of his own isn't actually all that shocking. And whilst that is a valid point, if I'm honest, I think the main reason that Simon didn't smile back at my beaming face was because it wasn't Simon's car that I was sitting in. This particular car, the one that I found myself sitting in, in the dark, belonged to an elderly, moustachioed Hungarian chap who was at this moment in time staring back at me with an expression of deep concern. To be fair, he had every right to be concerned. He'd only stopped to scrape some ice off his windscreen, but now he had a grinning nutter sitting in his car.

I mumbled an apology, he didn't have a clue what I said, I have no idea what he said, and I sheepishly made my retreat, back into Jack Frost's open arms.

So I'm still an idiot. Happy now?

This is what happens when we find ourselves alone in a chateau.

I live in Budapest

A snap of Liberty Bridge from one of our many walks

Junior seems to be fairly settled in her modest, all-inclusive studio apartment

Dancing with pink dancing sheep on the beaches of Kokomo (obviously)

[102]

Gellert Spa

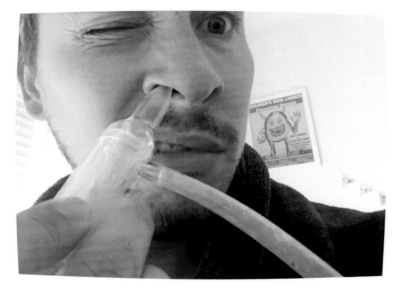

Hungarian nasal technology

Believe it or not, but this didn't cure my ingrowing toenail.

Katherine Jenkins meeting her idol, Mila Juno Hutchins in deepest, darkest Wales

Craving for rice milk.

Merry Christmas/Boldog Karácsonyt ya filthy animals!

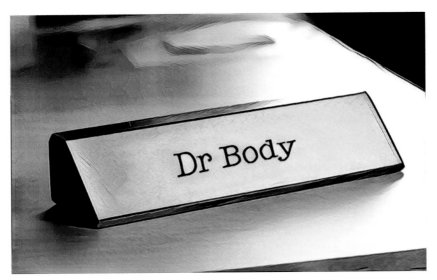

"Dr Body will see you now."

"What about *bitty*?" I ask.

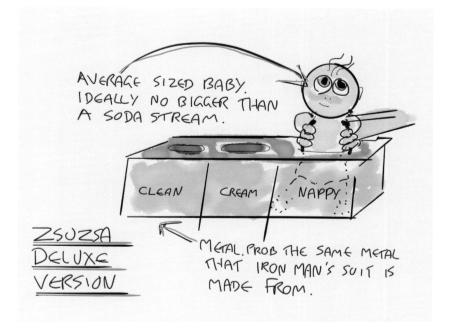

A Nappy Changing Machine!

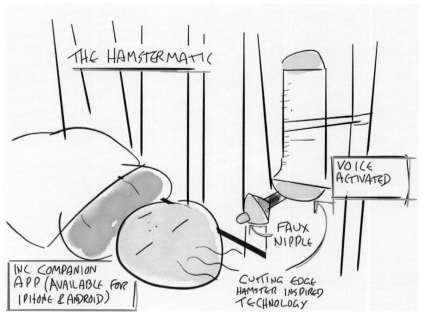

Coming to a shop near you, this Christmas

Easy Riders, Raging Baby

Birthday shenanigans at Istvandy Pinceszet

Apologies for ruining the photo by looking like an 1980's slime-ball.

Day 215

Spider-Dad

You may have read earlier about how becoming a father has made me soft. How it's turned me into a man who will let his heart strings be plucked willy-nilly. A man who will use the phrase 'willy-nilly'. A man who will go out of his way to give homeless men with frozen beards money to buy food, drink or a delicious hit of crack. A man who is now less of an all-round heartless swine than pre-baby Gareth was. But, what I previously failed to mention, is that I am now also Spider-Man. I know this may come as a shock to you as you had no idea that I was, in fact, Spider-Man. So I'll pause for a minute here to let you catch your breath. Go grab a camomile tea or something.

(PAUSE)

Are we good? Then I'll continue…

So I've actually suspected for some years now that I was a superhero, ever since I was involved in a car crash with a lorry on the M25 and my world momentarily clicked into slow motion. Well now, eight-odd years later my suspicions have been confirmed. Since the birth of our baby. I've been blessed with super reflexes to help compensate for my calamitous Daddying. Only last weekend in fact, I was carrying Mila in a Baby Björn baby-carrier. We got back to our dwelling and I pressed both of the release buttons on the carrier simultaneously. Somewhat surprisingly, the build up of tension and then its sudden release propelled Mila through the air like some kind of kamikaze baby-rocket, hurtling head-first towards the ground. But then my super-Dad reflexes kicked in and I calmly reached out and grabbed her little legs mid-air, saving her before impact.

I've also developed a fully-fledged, Dad-fuelled, spidey-sense. When danger's around I start to tingle. Rabid dog around the corner, sink hole up ahead, runaway train? No problem as Spider-Man here sees it before it happens. I'll give you an example. We went snowboarding a couple of days ago. We arrive at the ski resort and I'm debating internally whether or not to try and take Mila on a button lift with me. But then my spidey-sense kicks in. I'm tingling as my brain reminds me that I'm an absolute twat on button lifts. I just can't do them! They're my Everest! So I decide not to take Mila on a button lift, thereby preventing her from snowballing down a mountain when I inevitably fall. Astonishing foresight I'm sure you'll agree, and it's all due to my incredible spidey-sense.

Of course it's not all about me. Zsuzsa has a super-power of her own as well, as she has developed an innate ability to survive without sleep. Granted she often has an expression like a smacked arse as a result, but she gets by. But Super-Zsuzsa is a tale for another day. Let's get back to me being Spider-Man and a tale about me taking my new-found powers to the streets so that others outside of my little family can get a slice of my super-pie.

It's Tuesday. I've been working all day and I'm now on my way home to my beloved ladies. I'm listening to the La La Land soundtrack on full volume. Yeah! What a fucking rebel! I rise out of the illuminated Budapest Metro into a dark, cold and snowy evening. It must be about -15^0 Celsius so I pop my hat on and then cover that with the hood of my parker jacket and zip it up as far as it will go. I wander through the snowy streets looking like Kurt Russell from The Thing. I arrive at a crossing. It's here that my spidey-sense goes into overdrive as the only other person at the crossing is a small boy. I look around for his parents, but there's nobody near. I'm concerned for the child's safety. I mean of course I am! I'm Spider-Man! I stand there, wondering what to do whilst I wait for the green man. A few cars approach. I'm nervous as the small boy appears to be itching to cross the road. But what if he isn't yet skilled in the green cross code! Like all good super-heroes I decide to act.

I take a step forward and hold out my arm to stop the little boy running across the road to his certain doom. The small boy looks down at my arm. "Fear not young child!" I want to say, "For I am The Fucking Spider-Man!". But I don't, as I don't swear in front of young, impressionable minds and "The Fudging Spider-Man" sounds weird.

But then the small boy turns to face me, his saviour, and my jaw drops. He's not a small boy. He's a tiny adult man. Possibly a dwarf. He says something to me. I'm wearing headphones and have two further layers blocking my ear drums, but I get the gist. He's angry. If he had six other little fellas with him it would be easy to tell which one he was.

The green man appears and I hurriedly cross the road, whilst wishing that I could have been Batman instead.

Day 222

The Shit Storm

Mila, if you're reading this from the future, I apologise. Perhaps someone has dredged this up on your wedding day and decided to embarrass you. Perhaps that someone is me! To be fair it does sound like something I would do, and in that case I apologise again, but this week you've had diarrhoea. A lot of diarrhoea. Basically our week has been a huge tsunami of baby shit from start to finish and it all came out of your little baby butt.

It started just before we went away for a few days. I'm not at home, but I get a WhatsApp message from Zsuzsa...

"She just had a Niagara Falls of poo!"

I put two and two together and decide that Zsuzsa is talking about Mila, not her mother who she'd been speaking to earlier.

We'd planned to go away for a few days to visit the in-laws, and despite our worry that this is just the beginning of a vicious assault on our senses, we decide to stick to our plans.

A few shit-filled days later and we return home. It hits us instantly. A wall of stench.

"What the hell is that smell!?" asks Zsuzsa.

"Smells like someone's shat in our radiators!" I gasp.

"There must be a rogue shitty nappy somewhere in the flat."

Zsuzsa deduces.

And so we set to work. We search every nook and cranny of the flat. (I'm surprised as I previously didn't realise how many nooks that our flat had. I've often suspected that our flat had more than its fair share of crannies, but not so many nooks.) We search for about half an hour, find nothing, and eventually give up. We are beginning to accept that we will always live in a bog of eternal stench, but we're hoping that eventually, we will become accustomed to the smell. Dinner parties might be a hard sell though.

The next day, I escape from our cloud of shit particles and head to the office. A few hours later and I get another WhatsApp message from Zsuzsa...

"Her little bum is red and sore and her tummy is still upset. I'm using a camomile tea infused Muslim to wipe her butt."

I'm guessing the Muslim is probably equally as upset as Mila's tummy is, perhaps even more so. Zsuzsa will later accuse autocorrect, saying that she meant muslin (cloth), but I have my doubts. I'm blaming Donald Trump.

It's now Friday. We eventually found the rogue nappy (hiding in the bathroom bin). Mila is supposed to have a swimming lesson and to be fair her shit festival appears to be coming to an end, but just to be safe we decide to give swimming a miss. Instead, like some kind of wild, rock n' roll rebel, I've decided to pop Mila into her buggy and visit the local shopping centre to buy a pepper grinder.

Feeling like Iggy Pop I'm now in a kitchen utensil shop looking for pepper grinders, but something catches my eye. It's a massive glass piggy bank. I instantly decide that this is what is missing from my life. This is the item to complete our joyous existence. I pick the piggy bank up, pop it under my arm and head towards the counter. Being the conscientious Dad that I am, I look in the buggy to check on our little shitty cub. A glassy-eyed, motionless baby face stares back at me. I look closer. Still no movement. My heart begins to pound. I wave my free hand back and forth, millimetres from her face. Nothing.

"Oh my God! Mila!"

I'm panicking. With my free hand I slap her chubby little baby cheeks a few times. Mila turns and looks at me, a look of shock on her face. She had for some reason unbeknownst to me, decided to fall asleep with her eyes wide open. I was gentle with my slapping, but her expression tells me that this was not how she wanted to be roused from her slumber.

So, if you happened to be in a kitchen utensil shop in Budapest on Friday morning and saw a man, holding a massive piggy bank with one hand, whilst frantically slapping a baby with his other, that was me.

And Mila, I apologise again, this time for waking you up by slapping your little baby face, but now it's time for you to apologise. You need to apologise for sending me into a blind panic by sleeping with your goddamn eyes open in a kitchen utensil shop in Budapest on January 27th, 2017! Who the hell does that!?

Happy wedding day by the way. Enjoy the rest of 2046.

Day 229

When Raspberries Attack

We are standing in the kitchen trying to operate the coffee machine.

"Do you think Mila knows that some people are hairier than others?" asks Zsuzsa, through bleary eyes.

I ponder this question for a moment, my head pounding.

"That's an excellent question." I eventually reply.

"I mean, do you think she knows that you have more stubble than I do?" adds Zsuzsa, adding even more depth to this profound conundrum.

More pondering. Meanwhile we are making some serious headway with the coffee machine. We have located the ON button. Soon we will be knee-deep in glorious caffeine. After a minute or so of careful, measured consideration I'm ready to deliver my verdict.

"I think the answer is 'yes'."

Zsuzsa nods sagely, but then stops. She stares at me, her face now expressionless.

"What was the question again?" she asks.

My mind is blank.

"What question?" I reply.

We will later realise that we are in a state of sleep deprived delirium, and the most shameful part of this is that it was all self-inflicted. "How so!?", I hear you bellow. Isn't it obvious? It was all because I taught Mila how to blow raspberries. Master of my own destruction

Let me explain. Mila, our six-month-old little cub, is delighted with her newfound raspberry blowing skill and has really thrown herself headlong into her training, putting in some serious raspberry blowing hours. In fact she was blowing raspberries in our ears ALL NIGHT LONG, the cause of our sleep deprivation. I don't know if any of you have ever tried to sleep next to a baby on a raspberry-blowing mega-binge, but I'm here to tell you that it's a challenge. At least it was for me. On the rare moments that I did drop off, my dreams were soon invaded by a giant baby blowing raspberries on my belly, yanking me instantly back into the land of the conscious.

Sweet brown nectar is now pouring from a spout into a mug. Soon we will get the caffeine hit that our poor brains are pleading for. Soon we will be nearly twenty percent awake. Soon we will be in a state to begin rueing. We will be rueing raspberries like no man, woman or animal has ever rued a raspberry before. We will also notice, for the first time in our lives, that raspberry has a 'p' in it and wonder if we've been saying it wrong all these years.

It's later that day. Zsuzsa is in the bedroom with Mila.

"Honey! Honey! Come! Come quickly" Zsuzsa excitedly snorts.

I come running.

"What!? What is it?" I ask.

"I think Mila said Apa!"

This may sound like gobbledygook to non-Hungarians, but it's actually Hungarian for 'Dad'.

"Go on Mila!" says Zsuzsa. "Say Apa! Say Apa again!"

"I dare you! I double dare you mother-fudger!" I add in my head, with visions of Samuel L. Jackson from Pulp Fiction swirling around.

Mila just looks at her mother, then at me, and then at her mother. Something then dawns on me.

"Why would she say Apa?" I ask. "I don't call myself Apa. I call myself Daddy."

"I call you Apa when you're not here."

Ah! I see. A cunning plot to make my daughter speak Hungarian before she speaks English. I make a mental note to up my game and whisper English into her ear constantly when Zsuzsa isn't around.

Mila makes a sound.

"See!" exclaims Zsuzsa excitedly.

I'm not convinced. "It sounded more like 'potato'." I say. "Maybe she's asking for some potato?"

Nobody speaks for about thirty seconds. The only sound is the feint sound of our brains grinding to a halt.

"I find it strange that fat is yellow." exclaims Zsuzsa.

I look at her heavy eyelids. Mila blows a raspberry.

"More coffee?" I ask.

"More coffee."

Day 237

The Doghouse

I'm with Stew, a friend from London who's come to visit. We have arranged to play squash and we're currently making our way to our gladiatorial squash arena, where champions are forged. However, we're both feeling delicate, sorry for ourselves, and like a 1970's sitcom, we are both in 'The Doghouse'.

All because we got a bit too excited last night.

Let's quickly go back in time to the previous evening. A pre-Doghouse era when all was rosy with the world, and myself and Stew were just a lovable couple of 40-year-old half-wits…

We are all at a restaurant, and by 'all' I mean myself, Zsuzsa, Baby Mila, Stew and his beloved, Jen. Everything is very civilised. A piano player is tickling a Sinatra tune out of some nearby ivories, the lighting is soft, my steak is bloody and the red wine is quaffable. A couple of hours in and Mila, who's been exemplary up until now, decides that what this evening is missing is an excitable, high-pitched, squealing baby. So she begins to squeal. Zsuzsa and I try all of the anti-squealing tricks in our arsenal, but it's no use. Nothing is going to stop this runaway baby-squeal-train.

"I think I'll take Mila home." says Zsuzsa.

"I'll come with you." says Jen.

"I'll open the door for you." I add, ever the gent.

And just like that, all of the oestrogen in our little party heads home, leaving an imbalance of excitable half-wits alone and without supervision.

"Couple of beers?" says Stew.

"Why not." I reply.

It's now nearly two in the morning. "A couple of beers" seamlessly morphed into several beers, a few cocktails and a few gallons of palinka. We have just been kindly asked to leave a bar following an encounter in which Stew attempted to buy a man's hat and we are now in a taxi. We think we are heading back to my flat, but we are wrong. We are in fact heading towards The Doghouse.

So that was last night. Let's now go back to the beginning of this tale with Stew and I heading meekly towards a game of squash. We make it to the end of the road before realising that we will probably both die on the squash court and, deciding that we don't want to 'go out' like that, we decide to return home. We get back home, open the front door and our ladies are sitting there, staring at us. Judging us. We are sheepish. We look like two dogs who've stolen a couple of biscuits.

"Do you remember trying to engage our sleeping baby in conversation at two thirty in the morning?" Zsuzsa asks.

I do not remember this.

The rest of the morning is spent in grovel mode. We try to explain that we are just two men who got a bit over excited, went to a few bars, sampled the local produce and then tried to buy a stranger's hat, but it soon becomes apparent that we have a tough audience.

We eventually have a breakthrough when our ladies go for a massage, leaving us to look after the baby. A couple of hours later and they return home, like two relaxed lumps of well kneaded bread, their previous fury seemingly rubbed away by the fingers of tiny Thai ladies. Noticing this chink in their anger-armour we pounce upon our opportunity. We are like a pair of velociraptors working together, wheedling our ways back into their affections. Things are cleaned, tea is made, compliments bandied around, take-away collected etc. We are a pair of wheedle-raptors. It is clear to see that our wheedle display is masterful and should be turned into a training video for other Doghouse prisoners.

Later that night I'm lying in bed with Zsuzsa with our little cub nestled in between us. All is dark and all is silent, although if you listened hard enough you would be able to make out the distant sound of Zsuzsa's brain whirring. She is in deep thought.

"Mila will probably fly on a plane on her own at some point." Zsuzsa says.

"When?" I ask.

"When she's going to visit grandparents. She'll probably fly to Hungary, to the UK or Spain."

"I guess so." I reply.

"It'll be scary though." Zsuzsa remarks. "What if something happens to her when she's on her own?"

"Don't worry honey. Flights are pretty safe nowadays. Especially in Europe."

"But what if something did happen? I could never forgive myself."

Silence as we both contemplate the un-contemplate-able. Zsuzsa eventually breaks the silence.

"If anything happened, I'd kill myself."

I frown in the darkness.

"But what about me?" I reply.

"I'd kill you too." Zsuzsa replies without missing a beat.

We lie there in silence while I decide that the wheedle-training video might need to be put on the back-burner for a while.

Day 243

Dr Body

I'm at a doctor's surgery due to a renegade toenail, and the lady behind reception has just asked me for my mother's name. I'm a bit flummoxed.

"My mother's name?" I ask.

"Yes please." she replies.

"But I'm forty!"

"It's for security purposes." she says matter of factly.

"Security?"

"Yes."

I'm still confused. I didn't realise that my mother was such a big deal in Budapest. Although saying that maybe I should have twigged a few months back when my brother came over to visit. We went to the Sziget Music Festival and the people on the door wouldn't let him in until he'd dropped my mother's name. I thought it was a bit strange at the time, but now it all makes sense. My mother is obviously a big name in Budapest. Her name opens doors. All this time, I never knew.

I take a seat and wait. A few minutes pass.

"Girit."

"Girit!"

"Girit Hootkinsh!"

I turn around to see who this Girit fella is. Poor guy! He sounds like something that men in fluorescent jackets put on roads after heavy snow. A few seconds go by and nobody stands up. Slowly it begins to dawn on me that the receptionist is talking to me. I am the mysterious Girit. I am snowy road's worst nightmare.

"Uh, yes?" I say.

"Dr Body will see you now." replies the receptionist.

Dr Body! This is now my second favourite doctor's name after Dr Pop, the doctor who my wife often saw while she was pregnant. I'm now intrigued as to what will greet me behind Dr Body's door. Will it be a spandex-clad aerobics instructor from 1980's British breakfast television? Will it be a new villain from the Spider-Man universe? Will it be Elle McPherson, having recently graduated from Hungarian medical school?

I open the door and feast my eyes upon Dr Body. Somewhat disappointedly there's no spandex, no super-villain and no antipodean super-model. He's just an unassuming grey-haired Hungarian chap. He fixes me with a kindly gaze.

"Halo." he says.

"Halo." I reply.

"Angol?" (English) he asks.

"Yes!" I reply excitedly, relieved that I'm not going to have to put my Hungarian medical language knowledge to the test.

He beckons me to take a seat. I comply.

"What is problem?" he asks.

"My toe." I say. "I think I have an in-growing toenail."

He motions for me to remove my shoe and sock and I do. I mean, why wouldn't I? This is Dr Body! THE Dr Body! When Dr Body asks you to do something, you bloody well go and do it!

He studies my toe for a while, strokes his chin and then delivers his expert verdict.

"I think I am going to have to remove some of your knee." he says.

This is unexpected news.

"My knee?" I say, a little confused and also a tad concerned.

"Yes. Your knee. Just a little."

This has come as quite a shock. I didn't even realise anything was wrong with my knee. I'm also beginning to question this man's medical credentials. Maybe he's like one of those reflexologist people who think they can fix a sore throat by rubbing your little toe a bit. I decide to interrogate him.

"Are you a toe specialist?" I ask, in full David Frost mode.

"Toe specialist?" he replies. "No, no, no. Not toe specialist."

Hmmm. Zsuzsa told me I was seeing a toe specialist.

"No. My specialism is the anus!"

Wait. What?

"I go in the anus. My speciality is this. Anus specialist!" he says, a worrying twang of delight in his delivery.

Hmmm.

He beckons me to lie down. I do it because he is Dr Body, although I'm now a lot less enthusiastic in following his orders than I was a few moments ago. After all, I don't know what part of me is in the firing line. My toe? My knee? Maybe my beloved anus? I'm on edge, my eyes frantic as Dr Body pulls out a sharp instrument. I want my mother here with me. As a known face around Budapest she would ensure that no harm came to any of my parts. Dr Body spots my worry and he tries to relax me.

"Okay." he says. "I will just remove a little knee. No problem. Very little pain."

Nope. Still worried, although also relieved that my anus doesn't appear to be on the menu.

I'm like a frightened rabbit as Dr Body, as quick as a flash, grabs my foot, sprays freezing spray on my toe and cuts a piece of my toenail off. He shows me the bit of severed toenail.

"See. Just a little bit of knee."

I put my sock and shoe back on, covering up five of my ten tiny knees in the process, leave the surgery and hobble home to ask my beloved wife why she felt the need to send me to see an anus specialist.

Day 251
Ljubljana

"What about *bitty*?" I ask.

We're in a restaurant in Ljubljana (the capital of Slovenia). I've read that it's good to teach your baby words that they can associate with certain actions.

"No! No way! No bloody way!" replies Zsuzsa.

I use my heightened sense of perception that I've developed since becoming a Dad, read between the lines, and take it as a 'maybe' from Zsuzsa that she's okay with *bitty* being our chosen command word for breast feeding,

"Or *din-dins*?" I suggest, ever the helpful man.

"She's not a dog!"

The waiter appears.

"Are you ready to order?"

"Yes." I say. "I'd like the veal chops please and my wife would like the salmon."

By the way, she'd already told me this. I'm not a control freak like that fella from Fifty Shades of Grey (who I know is called Christian Grey, but think if I call him 'fella' it makes me sound like fractionally less of a loser).

"Very good." says the waiter, and turns to leave.

"Actually, one more thing." I say, stopping him in his tracks. I point at Zsuzsa. "Could I have my meal ten minutes before hers?"

The waiter looks at me like I'm some kind of insane, power-crazed husband who only allows his wife to eat once he's finished. He thinks I'm Donald Trump.

"It's so we can juggle the baby." I add, reading his muddled brain.

Seemingly satisfied, the waiter scurries off.

This staggered meal arrival plan is all part of our grand masterplan to allow us to carry on, more or less as normal, despite now being tasked with keeping a tiny, fleshy human alive. We are determined to still travel, and we are determined to still frequent restaurants. In order to do so, our restaurant-visiting process now goes a little something like this...

1. A scouting mission where one of us enters the restaurant beforehand to case the joint. In this scouting mission we assess the venue based on noise levels, ambience, buggy friendliness, toilet accessibility, likelihood of Mila approving of the decor, nappy-changing facilities and places to hide if our baby goes ape-shit.

2. Book a table at an unsociable hour, when pretty much nobody else is likely to be in the restaurant for dinner (i.e. 17:30).

3. Tip toe in, smiling at everyone apologetically for things that may happen in the future.

4. Sit down and take turns at inhaling our food while the other wanders around the restaurant with Mila.

5. Pull the rip cord and leg it when Mila starts to scream like a fox having sex.

6. Travel home with indigestion.

Now back to Slovenia.

Five minutes go by and my veal appears. I begin inhaling juvenile cow. Twenty seconds later and my young cow is gone. I fill the time before Zsuzsa's salmon arrives by necking wine like Oliver Reed. The salmon arrives, Zsuzsa hands me Mila and then sticks her face in her fish (not a euphemism). Mila is getting restless so I give her my phone to chew.

"How about *boob-time*?" I say.

"Nope." says Zsuzsa.

Hmmm.

"Map" says Mila.

"Here is the map." says Siri.

I look at our nearly seven-month-old baby girl in amazement.

"Mila just activated Siri on my iPhone and then said '*map*'!" I say.

"Well done!" says Zsuzsa.

"Maybe she's a genius!" I say.

Mila blows a raspberry and then begins to scream.

"Can we get the bill?" I holler.

Within two minutes we've abandoned ship and hit the mean streets of Ljubljana, young cow and fish fuelled indigestion raging in our bellies.

"I don't understand people who say they can't carry on as normal when they have a baby." I say. "We still travel! We still go to restaurants! Our life has hardly changed in that respect."

"I know." says Zsuzsa as we hurry back to our cramped hotel room, to ensure that we can all be in bed by seven o'clock on a Saturday night.

Day 258

The Wanderlusters

Venice Day 1

14:30   On route to Venice from Ljubljana. All three of us (Zsuzsa, Mila and I) are sick, sniffy, drugged-up messes. In fact, Zsuzsa has even called for a doctor (making full use of our travel insurance) to visit our hotel this evening to check out little Mila. The little blighter is coughing like a forty-a-day chain smoker.

15:15   We stopped off in a Slovenian village that sounds like *pyjamas* to take a look at some castle. The castle was amazing, but Mila didn't seem to be impressed. It takes more than a spectacular medieval castle carved into the side of a cliff face to pique the interest of this little diva. If it had nipples however, it might have been a different story.

17:43   Arrived in Venice. It's carnival time! Fuckety-fuckety-fuck! Sick people with a sick baby stuck in the middle of one of the biggest parties in Europe! Our suspicions were first aroused on boarding a boat. The other passengers were all male nuns, eighteenth century noble-men/women, human crows, six-foot-tall pussy cats or masked avengers.

18:47   Our hotel room is the size of a crisp packet.

19:45   The doctor arrived and Mila decided to spite us by pretending to be incredibly healthy for ten minutes. The doctor left, muttering in Italian. As soon as he left Mila once again decided to resemble a bubonic plague sufferer.

21:15　We can't go to the carnival due to our sickly child and snotty noses, but fear not as we've decided to bring the carnival to us. So, once Mila fell asleep we snuck off to our miniature bathroom and gorged on supermarket ham and cheese whilst drinking flat prosecco. Carnival! Carnival! Carnival!

Venice Day 2

10:30　Result! We asked for a cot to be put in our crisp-packet-sized room, but it didn't fit so the hotel moved us to another room. This one is like a Venetian palace! I will always ask for a cot in our room from now on. Even when Mila is in her thirties, she's coming on holiday with us and sleeping in a cot whether she likes it or not.

12:36　Zsuzsa, Mila and I were sitting outside a cafe in Venice. We were all still ill, all had little sleep, and subsequently were all tired. An imminent hit of caffeine was critical. The waitress was heading in our direction.

"Leave this to me honey." says Zsuzsa. "I know a tiny bit of Italian."

The waitress arrived.

"Dos cafe con leche por favor?" says Zsuzsa, in perfect Spanish.

The waitress paused for a moment before replying.

"We have cafe latte if that's okay?" she said in perfect English.

Zsuzsa thought for a moment, before turning to me.

"They have cafe latte." she said, speaking slowly so that I fully understand.

"That's good." I replied. "I'll have a cafe latte."

Zsuzsa turned to the waitress who was standing in between us and said, "He'll have a cafe latte. I will too. Two cafe lattes please."

"No problem." replied the waitress.

Zsuzsa again turned to me and gave me a reassuring look. A look that exuded confidence. A look that reassured me. A look that said "I've got this."

What would I do in Venice without my master of communications?

17:50   We've spent the rest of the day wandering around this phenomenal city, surrounded by grown-ups dressed as animals. Just when Mila thought she had it all figured out, we've taken her to Venice during Mardi Gras. Thankfully she appeared to love every second of it! I don't think I've ever seen her smile as much! In order to fit in I decided to buy a mask. Zsuzsa decided not to, instead preferring to flaunt her naked face to all of the Venetians. The poor lamb looked ridiculous without a mask.

18:14   Top Venice Tip! - If you visit Venice with a baby, make sure you bring a baby carrier! Clambering over all of those bridges with a buggy would be a pain in the rectum.

20:38   Mila has just fallen asleep. We are eating take-away pizza in our bathroom. I'm sitting on the toilet quaffing wine. La dolce vita.

Venice Day 3

10:30   I was enjoying a bidet today when I suddenly heard a yelp. I ran into our bedroom to see Zsuzsa and Mila both in tears. Mila had decided to hurl herself, headfirst off the bed. Thankfully, no damage done. Can't a man enjoy a bidet in peace anymore without babies falling off things!?

10:35   Maybe Mila is a lemming.

11:14   With Mardi Gras finished we venture outside again. Not a grown-up dressed as an animal in sight! Venice is incredible! We love it. Mila is also seemingly much better too. If only they'd had Calpol in 1665! We celebrate in time honoured fashion by buying a ukulele. Tomorrow we head to Bled

Bled Day 1

14:12   Lovely big, tranquil lake. Nothing much to report here although we're the only people staying in a massive hotel. Again! The air here seems to send Mila to sleep. I'm going to try and gather a load in a plastic bag and take it home.

02:32   Woken up from a nightmare! Mila was playing the music from Deliverance on a ukulele.

Austria Day 1

16:05   Just arrived in Austria, fulfilling our plans to end our European Vacation with a little skiing/snowboarding adventure. We've rented an apartment in a guesthouse and are joined by friends of ours from Budapest, Thomas and Adri.

17:54   Mila was having her nappy changed earlier. Being the wriggly cub that she is, she flipped herself over on to her belly just as Adri walked in. She took one look at Mila's naked, chubby little butt and equally naked and chubby little legs and said.

"She looks just like her father."

I don't know how to take that. I might re-join the gym.

Austria Day 2

14:02   A bodacious morning of snowboarding before relieving Zsuzsa of baby-handling duties. Apparently Mila has just started sitting up on her own.

18:35   We think Mila is calling me "BA!" and Zsuzsa "Aaaaa-waaa!".

18:46   I've just done a quick search and apparently "Ba" is Vietnamese for "father"! Mila's bloody Vietnamese!

Budapest - Home

20:21   I've just driven my girls across Austria, Slovenia and Hungary to reach our nest in Budapest. Despite the fact that we've all been ill from start to finish; despite the fact that our (first) Venice hotel room was the size of a baked potato; despite the fact that I apparently have the arse and legs of a baby; and despite the fact that the radio station that we were listening too on our five-and-a-half hour journey home played *Agadoo*, not once, not twice, but three times, we've had an amazing week and a bit. Zsuzsa and I were worried initially that having a baby would kerb our travelling fun, but it's actually surprisingly easy as long as we plan ahead, time things to fit in with Mila's rhythm and carry half the contents of our flat around with us at all times. We've also noticed the biggest leaps in Mila's developments every time we go away. Having just got home, the change in her from eleven days ago is remarkable. She's crawling, sitting up and just seems far more at ease with herself. She also seems to love visiting new places. From the looks of it Mila has inherited our wanderlust genes. We need to plan our next trip!

20:32   Just been trying to check out my arse and legs from behind in a mirror.

"Looks just like her father!"

Bugger off!

Day 266
Goulash

"I think the pigeons are bigger in Budapest!" exclaims my mother.

She's come to Budapest to visit, and we (myself, my mother, her husband Tony and Mila) are sitting outside a restaurant near the riverbank. My mother's currently staring at a gang of medium-sized pigeons which, as you've probably guessed, she thinks look big. Earlier today she told me that the ants look smaller.

The waiter approaches.

"What can I get you?" he asks in perfect English.

I'm confident that mother dearest is going to order a cup of tea as her bloodstream must now be running dangerously low on cup-of-tea levels (i.e. 20% blood, 80% tea). She's even brought some emergency teabags with her to Budapest. Just in case.

"Can I have the vegetable soup?" asks my mother.

I'm gobsmacked.

"Goulash for me." says Tony.

"Egy nagy tál guyásleves és egy nagy pohár hazi vörös haj." I say.

The waiter pauses for a moment to process my sentence. He looks a tad confused, but then seems to twig and wanders off.

"You speak very good Hungarian!" my mother says. "I'm very impressed!"

I smile proudly and decide not to mention the fact that I think I've just ordered a large glass of house red hair.

A few minutes later and our orders arrive. This is Mila's cue. Prior to this moment she's been sitting quietly, chewing on her toy giraffe and observing. Now however, she appears to be being burnt alive by invisible acid. She's either hungry or she's just realised that the woolly hat that my mother has knitted, is actually for her. I look around and sheepishly smile at the other diners. I take Mila out of her buggy and sit her on my knee, but it's no good. She's still wailing like her uncle was when he found out that they were cancelling Birds of a Feather..

"Maybe she'd like some vegetable soup?" suggests my mother.

"Hmmm." I say. "I'm not sure Zsuzsa will approve."

"AAAAAAAAARRRRRRGGGGGHHHHH!!!" screams Mila.

"Give me the soup." I say and begin shoveling spoonfuls of the stuff down Mila's throat. The soup runs out yet Mila is still restless. A few additional spoonfuls of goulash however, seem to do the trick.

"Don't tell mummy." I whisper to Mila.

She looks at me as though I'm an idiot. "I can't even speak you twat!" her face says. "How the bloody hell am I going to tell Mummy!?"

I begin attempting to eat my goulash with Mila on my knee, although her grasping little, soup-loving baby hands are making things

[138]

tricky.

"Do you want me to hold her while you eat?" asks Tony.

I throw Mila at him, pick up my soup bowl like a mug and begin gulping. Once the soup has been downed I then neck my glass of red wine (which thankfully doesn't appear to be that hairy).

In the meantime, Mila has found a bread bowl to play with and appears to be momentarily calm. I start to relax.

"Zsuzsa's going to the ballet tomorrow." I say.

"What's she going to see?" asks Tony.

"Carmen something."

"Carmen Miranda?" asks Tony, and then roars with laughter. I laugh also, although I have no idea what we're laughing at.

"Maybe." I mutter under my breath, barely audible.

We leave the restaurant and begin our journey home.

We are walking past a backdrop of the Danube and Buda Castle. My mother gets her camera phone out.

"Could you just go and stand over there?" she asks. "I just want it to look like we're having lots of fun."

My aunt is also on holiday at the moment. My mother is determined to show her that we are having more fun than she is. She takes the photo and we walk on.

"I think the buildings are taller here." says my mother.

"I think it's because you don't usually look up." says Tony.

"I do usually look up!"

"Hmmm." says Tony.

We walk on towards my flat. Mila has fallen asleep. I'm secretly Googling Carmen Miranda.

"I quite fancy a cup of tea," says my mother.

There you go.

But I don't. Instead I meekly hand Mila back to Zsuzsa. She looks at her mummy and smiles.

What the hell! What is this treachery!?

"She was making funny noises in her sleep. Maybe she had a nightmare." suggests Zsuzsa. "Maybe you did something bad to her in her dreams?"

"Like what?" I ask.

Zsuzsa thinks for a moment.

"Maybe you murdered me." she says, before turning to Mila, smiling and saying "Did Daddy kill Anya (Hungarian for Mum)? Was Daddy a bad, murderous man?"

I'm aghast. I rarely do anything to suggest that I could be a cold-blooded murderer.

"But why? Why would she think I'd kill you?" I ask.

Zsuzsa again thinks for a moment. This is the second time now in a matter of minutes. A possible record.

"Maybe it's because you've been trying to teach her Al Pacino impressions? Maybe she doesn't want to do an impression of Al Pacino?"

This is true. Over the last few days I've been trying to teach Mila to do an Al Pacino impression. I've begun with something simple, "Hoo hah!" from Scent of a Woman. Once she's mastered this I plan to move on to something a little more complex. Something like "She's got a GRRREEEEAAAAATTTT ASS!" from Heat. Obviously, like

Day 272

The Fever

I'm being shaken.

"Wake up! Honey! Wake up!"

Zsuzsa is standing above me. I'm confused. It's dark and I glance at the clock. It's 01:36. Why has my wife woken me up at this ungodly hour? There are only two possible explanations that I can think of. Either something is wrong or she's horny.

Who am I kidding? Something's wrong.

"What's up?" I ask.

"Mila's really hot. Can you come and have a look?"

Zsuzsa and Mila are currently sleeping in the nursery. Up until a few days ago Mila had slept in our room alongside us. We're trying now to transition her into her own room and Zsuzsa's sleeping in the spare bed in the nursery to help everything go smoothly. This is amazing news for me! After just one night alone I have de-aged about four years! I'm like Benjamin Button! At this rate I'm going to hit puberty in reverse in just over a week's time. I'm not thrilled about the idea of my balls retracting back up into my body, but anyway. Back to the story.

We're now in the nursery. I'm still half asleep.

"Touch her honey. She's so, so, so hot!" says a concerned

Zsuzsa.

I put my hand on Mila's head and I instantly know why Zsuzsa felt the need to wake me from my precious beauty sleep. Mila is hot. Very hot. If I balanced a hard boiled egg on her forehead, within seconds it would be too hard for soldiers.

"Have you checked her temperature?" I ask.

"I tried, but I'm not sure if the thermometer is working. It says she's only 35! That can't be right! She's hotter than the sun!"

This does indeed sound suspect. I see the thermometer resting on the bedside table, decide to stress test it and pop it into my mouth.

Zsuzsa is stroking the back of our groggy, semi-conscious little baby girl.

"Do you think I should call the doctor?" asks Zsuzsa.

"Yes." I say out of the corner of my mouth.

Zsuzsa looks up at me. A look of surprise appears on her face.

"What are you doing!?" she says.

"Seeing if the thermometer's working." I reply, still feeling sleepy.

"Honey! That's an anal thermometer!"

My eyes widen as the words sink in and I'm suddenly more awake than I've ever previously been. I spit the thermometer out.

"Noooooooooo!" I whisper-scream.

"What the fuck honey!?" says Zsuzsa, whilst positioning Mila on to all fours.

Mila stirs and looks up at me with her flushed, chubby cheeks glowing in the darkness. She looks confused as our eyes meet. She is no doubt wondering why my eyes are full of both regret and horror.

"I'm just going to give her this suppository." says Zsuzsa.

Mila and I are still staring into each other's eyes as the suppository is inserted. Now it's Mila's turn for her eyes to widen. She turns around to look at her Mummy, a 'WTF' look on her little baby face.

(As an aside, what is it with Hungarians and their obsession of administering things anally? What's wrong with the good old mouth?)

Zsuzsa puts Mila's nappy back on and hands her to me.

"I'm going to call the doctor." she says.

Zsuzsa gets up to leave the room. I follow her with Mila in my arms.

"Where are you going?" asks Zsuzsa.

"To clean my teeth." I say.

"Honey! Don't take her out of the room. She'll be wide awake!"

"But…"

"Please honey!"

I sit down in the dark with Mila. Mila is struggling to stay awake. I think she is also trying to stay as far away as possible from my breath. In the other room I hear Zsuzsa on the phone, whispering

[143]

in Hungarian.

A few minutes later and she returns. She looks furious.

"What did the doc say?" I ask.

"She told me that all good mothers should keep three forms of medicine with them at all times to control their babies temperature!"

Usually I'd be angry at this, but it's funny how putting a thermometer in your mouth that had only moments before been up a babies anus can give you a new perspective on things.

"Did she say if we should be worried?" I ask.

"No. Says it's normal and probably because she's teething. Told me not to worry."

I touch Mila's forehead. The suppository seems to be doing the trick as she now feels much cooler.

Comforted by this news I bid my ladies goodnight, point myself in the direction of the mouthwash, and leave the room. In the morning I will order one of those thermometers that you point at foreheads.

Day 279

Men Who Stare at Wolves

"Cheeky!?"

"Yes."

"Dr Cheeky!?"

"Yes."

"DR CHEEKY LASZLO!?"

"YES!"

We are driving through the countryside. Zsuzsa has just informed me that the surgeon who will be operating on my toe in a few days' time is called Dr Cheeky. Naturally, I'm ecstatic. I thought my life had peaked when I met Dr Body, but then along came Dr Cheeky!

I roar with laughter. Zsuzsa stares at me in bemusement.

"What!?" asks Zsuzsa.

"That name!" I say. "It's amazing! What is it with Hungarian doctors? Dr Cheeky! Dr Body! Dr Pop! Why do they all sound like sugary, carbonated drinks!?"

"It's spelt C-S-I-K-Y." says Zsuzsa.

I ignore her. She's obviously desperate to drag me down from my all-time life high of finding Dr Cheeky. If I block her voice out for just a minute I can continue to spell Dr Cheeky any way that I goddamn please.

We continue our drive through the countryside in silence. We are heading back to our baby girl after visiting the spa and we are both incredibly tired as Mila has been ill for the last few days with bronchitis. In fact, only last night, I was awoken by Mila projectile-vomiting on me at 02:42 in the morning. I lay there shell-shocked and covered in regurgitated peach while Mila sat next to me, grinning like a Cheshire cat and clapping like a circus seal (her latest trick). It was like a scene from some kind of budget "I'm a Celebrity, Get Me Out of Here!". But despite this horrific moment being so raw in my memory, and despite the incredible fatigue that we are both currently feeling, I have a big fat smile on my face. All thanks to Dr Cheeky.

We turn a corner. That's odd. There's a car parked on a bend in a very precarious position. I slow the car down to navigate past.

"Oh my God!" shouts Zsuzsa.

"What!? What!? What!?"

"Wolves!" she squeals.

"Wolves?"

"Yes Wolves! In the woods! Wolves in the woods! Those people had stopped to take photographs of them!"

"You're joking?"

"Nooo! There were wolves! In the woods!"

We continue to drive on, away from the wolves as my tired

mind processes what she's just told me.

"You're absolutely sure that there were wolves?"

"Yes!" Then I remember something. Last year I read an online article that said that packs of wolves had been known to creep into Hungary from Slovakia, with various sightings in the Bükk mountains over the last few years. We are in the Bükk mountains! I put two and two together. WOLVES! I begin slowing down.

"What are you doing?" asks Zsuzsa.

"Looking for somewhere to turn around." I say.

"Honey! We've got to get back to Mila! I told my parents we'd be back soon."

"We will. This'll only take a minute."

"Honey!"

"Look. I've never seen wolves in the wild before. We've got to turn around!"

"But we need to bath Mila!"

"Two minutes isn't going to make a difference. I'll bath her really fast. Wolves honey! Bastard wolves!"

I find a space to turn around and begin the journey back to the wolf hot-spot. I'm digging my heels in here. Last night we drove past a field that was on fire and Zsuzsa wouldn't let me stop to take a selfie.

"Are you absolutely sure they were wolves?"

"YES!"

We crawl along slowly, eyes peeled for any sign of wild dog gang.

"Have you got the camera ready?" I ask.

Zsuzsa nods. This is amazing. I'm tingling with excitement. I feel like David Attenborough! We are now very close to the spot where my eagle-eyed wife first spotted the canine beasts. We are crawling along in stealth mode, camera phones at the ready...

Goats.

Day 288

The Armada

I'm in a little village in Andalusia for my Dad's 70th birthday. I'm sitting at a table outside a bar with various members of my family (Zsuzsa, Mila, my Dad, my brother and my nephew). There are also two other people sitting at our table. A woman from Blackburn and her Irish husband who've invited themselves to sit with us. The Irish guy has just said something that has caught my attention. I decide to question it.

"You have ten metres of metal in your head?" I ask.

"Yes." he proudly responds.

"Ten metres?" I again ask, just to be sure that I've heard this correctly.

"Yes! Ten metres!" he replies.

I look around at everyone else, just to check that I'm not the only one surprised at this fact. Everyone else seems to have taken it as gospel. Still I'm unsure. Ten metres seems a lot. Especially given the size of his head. I look at it again. It looks five metres wide at best. I'm about to continue my line of Paxman-esque inquisition when Zsuzsa stops me in my tracks by announcing her departure. I mean from the evening. Despite what you may think, she's not an airplane

"Why are you heading back? It's not even nine." I say.

"It's getting a bit cold." Zsuzsa replies. She then gets up and, like a Boeing 747, promptly leaves with my baby.

I glance at my brother Ross. He's whispering with my Dad. They both smile, nod and turn to face me.

"What?" I ask.

"Ross recognised it as well." my father says.

"Recognised what?" I respond.

"The syndrome."

I stare at them blankly before my father adds, "First child syndrome."

I instantly see what's going on here. These clowns are calling us neurotic!

"Hang on. We're not neurotic parents!"

Ross smiles at me smugly.

"You'll learn." he says.

I bristle.

"But we're not!" Sometimes Mila doesn't even wear socks!" I say indignantly.

"It's nothing to be ashamed of." Ross says. "Most parents are like it. Even *we* were like it once! Then you have a second child and realise that you were worrying unnecessarily."

Ross then sits back, takes a sip of beer.

"Just chill out." he says. "Don't worry about them. They'll be okay."

He then attempts to locate his child via his phone using the tracking device that he's attached to him. He eventually finds him standing behind him.

The woman from Blackburn starts telling me a story about how she got "rat-arsed" the night that Blackburn won the Premier League in the mid-nineties. It's time to leave. I finish my drink and out of the corner of my eye witness my Dad hurl his six-and-a-bit-year-old grandson into a pub chair, skewering him on the chair leg. Theo runs to Ross in tears. Ross looks at my Dad.

"Sorry. I didn't mean to do that! We were play-fighting! He slipped!"

Ross consoles his crying child and we make our way back.

Two minutes later and my Dad has found an orange on the floor. Theo is riding on Ross's shoulders. My Dad, feeling bad, decides to engage Theo in a bit of harmless ball/orange game fun. He hurls the orange at Theo. It hits him on the nose. Theo screams.

"Dad!" says Ross.

"Sorry! I didn't mean to do that! It was going to miss, but he moved his nose with pace towards the orange!"

"Please stop beating up my son." pleads Ross.

"I'll try." says Dad.

We walk home. Once there I check Mila's socks haven't come off in bed, and fall asleep dreaming of ten metre wide metal heads

Day 293

Naughty

Mila's suddenly become very naughty. I don't know how or when this happened, but there's suddenly a mischievous glint in her eye and a seeming desire to destroy. It seems to have coincided with her new found ability to crawl, pull herself up and climb.

I've spent the last few days frantically baby-proofing our home in a desperate attempt to prevent our eight-month-old baby from cutting her face open on one of our home's several sharp corners. It's only now that I have a mobile baby (and by this I mean a baby who can move around on her own, not a novelty mobile phone) that I realise what a death trap our home is. There's danger at every corner. It's only now that I see our home for what it really is. The ancient, booby trapped temple from the start of Raiders of the Lost Ark.

I've just finished Mila-proofing our razor sharp coffee table by covering its edges in soft, spongy foam. I sit back and admire my handiwork. Mila also seems to be full of admiration. She crawls towards the table and runs her baby hands across the protective softness, her eyes wide in appreciative wonder.

Mila turns to me and smiles.

I stand there proudly. That's right, baby girl. I did that for you. I made it soft for *you*. All because I love you and don't want to have to rush you to the hospital with blood gushing from a gaping wound.

Mila returns her gaze to the coffee table. Suddenly that mischievous glint appears. She clenches her gums, yanks on the cushioned pad with all her might and tears it from the coffee table.

"You little shit!" I say in exasperation.

"Honey!" says Zsuzsa, appearing apparently from thin air. "Don't speak to her like that. She'll pick up on your anger and it'll affect her."

"But she's like one of those bloody baboons that tear your windscreen wipers off at safari parks!" I mutter, frustrated.

"She's just a baby. She doesn't know what she's doing."

I look at Mila. She's now sitting next to the table, looking like an innocent angel chewing on protective foam. She smiles at me. She knows what she's doing. She's rubbing my nose in it.

"And please try not to speak to her with a negative tone. Her mind is very impressionable at the moment. If you're angry with her she won't grow up to be the professional tennis-playing, ballet-dancing, kung-fu-fighting, award-winning scientist and successful writer that you want her to be." adds Zsuzsa.

It's true. This is what Mila is going to be. A professional tennis-playing, ballet-dancing, kung-fu-fighting, award-winning scientist and successful writer. She has no say in the matter.

"I don't think me calling her 'a little shit' is going to do anything. It's not going to make her become a pole-dancing bank robber or anything." I reply.

"You never know." says Zsuzsa. "Best to play it safe."

It's now several days later. We're on a plane flying back from Spain. So far Mila has been a very good little lady. She's given me a few 'hand-off's' to the face when I attempted to kiss her cheek, but that's about it, and maybe that's more related to the sausage that I've been eating than anything else.

Zsuzsa is by the window, I'm in the middle seat and a Slovakian woman who has more than her fair share of nose is sitting to my left. Mila is on my lap, taking a breather in between breast feeds (our way of sedating Mila on flights).

"What a cute baby." says the Slovakian lady.

"Thanks" I reply.

Mila fixes the Slovakian lady with an adorable smile. The Slovakian lady's heart melts, she smiles back and leans in, inches from Mila's face. Suddenly something changes in Mila's face. It's subtle and the uninitiated wouldn't have recognised it, but I do. I've seen that look before. The glint. The mischievous glint.

"Back off Slovakian lady!" I want to say, but I'm not quick enough.

With the speed of a spider monkey, Mila reaches out and grabs the Slovakian lady's bulbous nose. The Slovakian lady suppresses a squeal as Mila applies surprising force to her grab. I try to pull Mila away, but she clings on with freakish strength and the Slovakian lady's face comes with her. The Slovakian lady and myself (with my one free hand) attempt to prise Mila's fingers from the increasingly scarlet nose. Eventually we are successful and the Slovakian lady sits back and tries to compose herself.

[154]

"I'm so sorry." I say. "She's going through a bit of a naughty phase."

"Don't worry about it." says the Slovak, trying her best to act nonchalant, but with the colour of her nose betraying her.

I keep our naughty little lady away from strangers' noses for the remainder of the flight. She's got a long way to go to becoming a professional tennis-playing, ballet-dancing, kung-fu-fighting, award-winning scientist and successful writer, but we'll get there.

Day 299

Indiana Jones and The Easter Egg Hunt

I'm in a small village, in the middle of the Hungarian wilderness, partaking in an Easter egg hunt. Mila is asleep. Zsuzsa is charging around the village like an Hungarian Anneka Rice. She is determined to not only defeat her opponents (small Hungarian children), but to leave them shattered, broken and forever destroyed.

"Come on honey! Speed up! We only have an hour!" she bellows.

I speed up. What choice do I have faced with such a force of nature.

"Wait here!" commands Zsuzsa, before sprinting across a road towards a kindergarten.

I can do nothing, but stand and wait. Mila is snoring. A few minutes later and I see a blur of strawberry blonde hair heading my way. It's Zsuzsa. She's holding an egg.

"Come on! We have to get to the castle!" she barks.

And so off we go. Zsuzsa is jogging. I'm in hot pursuit with a sleeping baby in a push chair. This is what Easter is all about! This is what Jesus would have wanted! We're at the castle and before I know what's happening Zsuzsa has another egg.

"Come on honey! We have to get the third egg!" screams Zsuzsa, and off we go.

We are bounding through the village with frightening speed, but suddenly Zsuzsa slows. An obstacle! It's an old lady selling quince jelly, the oldest trick in the book, and my beloved wife has fallen for it!

"Honey! What are you doing?" I ask.

"This lady's selling quince jelly!" says Zsuzsa. "We should buy some."

"But the egg hunt! What about the egg hunt?!" I implore.

I'm desperately trying to snap my wife out of her quince jelly trance. She can't see this for what it is. The old lady, she's the Hungarian village equivalent of a siren and Zsuzsa is a young sailor!

"Honey!" I say again. "We don't have much time!"

But it's no use. Zsuzsa is distracted. I then catch a glimpse of the old quince-jelly-selling lady's feet and suddenly I'm distracted too. She's wearing socks with sandals! Several minutes pass, before I snap out of it.

"Honey!"

I have Zsuzsa's attention again. She has no memory of how it happened, but she's now clutching some quince jelly! Through the village we go.

Suddenly I'm aware of a presence. A couple with a small child in a buggy have appeared, as if from nowhere, on our right shoulder. COMPETITORS! They're trying to hide it, but I see their game.

They're travelling at an unnatural speed and there's only one reason for people to move that quickly through an Hungarian village! They are fellow egg hunters! Our nemesis!

I'm now torn. On one hand my competitive genes want to speed up and very gradually overtake these jokers in a nonchalant manner, but I'm British and also don't want to appear to give a shit! I look at the couple and assess them. I can't deny that I'm full of admiration for their impressive turn of pace, but the woman, she's a big girl! She can't keep this up for ever. I decide that she will fade soon and that our superior stamina will come into play.

Two eggs later and I'm proved right as we cruise past our sweaty, puffing competitors, but Zsuzsa seems frustrated. Part of this egg hunt is finding the eggs, but another part is deciphering cryptic, Hungarian word clues. So far, all of them seem to be very floral in their nature.

"These bloody clues!" an exasperated Zsuzsa gasps. "They're all hard-core botanical bullshit!"

"Show me." I say.

Zsuzsa shows me. I look at the pictures of Hungarian flowers and the various cryptic word clues. I realise that even if they were in English I would be of no use.

"Uh." I say.

Zsuzsa sighs.

"You should really work on your Hungarian botanical vocabulary!" she says.

I make a mental note to do so.

It's about thirty minutes later. We've just found the final egg! I check the watch. We have eight minutes to get back to base camp (a small Hungarian school hall). This is going to be tight!

"I'll go ahead! says Zsuzsa. "You follow!"

And with that she sprints off into the horizon, clutching six, small plastic eggs. What a woman!

Despite the odds being stacked against her, her impressive turn of pace meant that my beloved wife made it in the nick of time, and out of seventy five teams, miraculously, we won! As we drive back through the Hungarian countryside, Zsuzsa clutches the spoils of victory (a tiny bag of small chocolate eggs). She's beaming.

"You know honey, I don't think I've ever felt more like Indiana Jones than I did today." she says.

I smile back at my brave explorer, my adventurer, my destroyer of small Hungarian children's dreams and I can't help but feel proud.

So, Steven Spielberg, if you're reading this and interested in snapping up the film rights for Indiana Jones 5, please feel free to give me a call.

Happy Easter.

Day 306

The Cleaner

"Honey, please make sure that the flat is tidy for the cleaner." says Zsuzsa, as she leaves the flat to visit the dentist.

"But isn't that what we pay her for?" I reply.

But it's no use. The front door has already been closed and Zsuzsa has already deserted me with a messy-ish flat and a (nearly) nine-month-old baby. I scan the scenery to decide where I should begin. Should it be with the toys scattered all over the living room floor, my 'floordrobe' of clothes, or the aftershock of the baby food explosion that surrounds the baby feeding chair?

"BA!" says Mila.

I couldn't have put it better myself.

The truth is that, despite the ridiculous additional work that comes with cleaning for a cleaning lady, I do enjoy the fact that we employ a cleaning lady to visit once a fortnight. Even if the flat is so spotless that all she need do is sit on the sofa and watch Hungarian soaps for two hours, it would still be worth it as it makes me feel as though I'm in Downton Abbey and have my own 'staff'.

I actually used to get the same, warm, fuzzy feeling back in London when a friend would stay once a fortnight and repay our kindness of a bed for the night, by cooking us a meal. He was probably unaware of this, but in my mind at least, he was our cook and our spare room was his quarters.

Anyway, eventually, after about an hour of furious cleaning, the cleaning lady arrives and begins dusting our spotless shelves. Mila looks at me. I know that look. She feels in the way and assumes that I am feeling the same. You know what? The perceptive, fleshy little cub is right! I gaze out of the window at the Buda Hills. It's a sunny day and I decide that we'll make ourselves scarce with a little stroll around a nearby island (Margit Sziget). I attach our baby carrier to my person, pop Mila in, fasten it shut and we set off on an adventure.

Ten minutes later and we're on a tram heading to Margit Sziget. I can't help but notice that lots of ladies, and even a few men are flashing smiles in our direction. Most people might assume that the smiles are all due to the cute little lady strapped to my chest, but I know better. It's because I'm wearing my new jumper. It's obviously a hit.

We're now on Margit Sziget, strolling around the island. I'm initially disappointed as the luscious green island now appears to be a building site. I scan the horizon. Diggers, builders, trucks, holes, rubble and security tape blot the landscape, as far as the eye can see. I momentarily consider turning back, but then snap out of it. After all, would Columbus have turned back if he'd arrived in America only to be greeted with JCB diggers? No way Jose!

We're about five minutes into our stroll through the construction site when I decide that now would be an idyllic moment to take Mila out of her carrier, sit on a bench, feed her apple juice and find a spot to stare at, which isn't full of builder's bum cracks. I reach behind to unfasten the carrier…but…this isn't good. I can't reach the clip! I try again, but it's no use. I can't reach it. My stupid, inflexible shoulders are thwarting me!

"What is this bullsh…erbert?" I say.

Mila has no answer.

I'm standing in a building site with a baby strapped to me, and I can't shake her off. This must be what it's like to have a leech! I attempt to call Zsuzsa, but there's no answer. Panic is rising. My mind is racing. What if Zsuzsa goes missing? Granted it'd be a huge blow if my beloved wife disappeared. I'd be devastated! Not least because I'd have no-one to un-attach this baby from my chest. What if Mila and I are stuck together for years!? I mean, I love Mila and all of that crap, but I wouldn't be able to go and see 18 rated films in the cinema until 2035! What if I need to wait until she grows enough that her feet touch the ground and we're able to work on the problem as a team? But how will she go to school to learn the necessary skills to help free us? Would I need to go too? The last thing I want is to go through the education process in Hungary with my baby. No, there's only one thing for it. I'll have to home- school her. Alternatively, do I ask one of these hairy builders to help free my baby? I doubt that they speak English. How could I mime it? They might think I'm asking for them to scratch my back! I don't want my back scratched by a hairy builder, Hungarian or otherwise!

My phone rings. It's Zsuzsa. Phew.

"What's up?"

Twenty minutes later, Zsuzsa arrives. My heroine! Like some kind of modern-day Joan of Arc, she unclips the fastener, myself and Mila are free, and our happy family of three stroll through the dystopian wasteland, as though this nightmare had never happened.

Day 311

The Yuppie

We are running dangerously low on Nespresso capsules. As I'm sure you can imagine, as a result, the mood at home is extraordinarily sombre.

"What are we going to do?" asks Zsuzsa, fighting back the tears.

I'm trying not to panic although this is obviously a very stressful time. A brainwave hits me.

"Why don't I buy some more tomorrow? I can pop to the Nespresso shop on Andrássy Avenue after work?"

At this suggestion, I can visibly see hope returning to Zsuzsa's face. She doesn't say it, but I know what she's thinking.

"Bloody hero! Bring me those capsules and I will ravish your body!"

It's now tomorrow. I've encountered a slight obstacle to my plans as I'd forgotten that I'd planned to meet a friend named Rupert at Brody Studios, the private members club that I'm a member of. There's a story-telling evening on and we'd agreed to meet straight after work, leaving little time for coffee shopping. But then I remember Zsuzsa's haunted, Nespresso-deprived face, and despite the tight schedule, I decide that I've enough time to squeeze in a trip to the Nespresso store before heading to Brody Studios.

I'm outside the Nespresso store when my phone buzzes. It's a message from Rupert.

"Where the devil are you?" it reads.

"Just picking up some Nespresso capsules." I reply.

A few seconds later and I get a response.

"Bloody yuppie!"

I stare at my phone screen. Yuppie!? What's so yuppie about Nespresso capsules? They're just tiny pods of coffee granule heaven! That's all! Nothing more! Yuppie!? How dare he! I haven't been this outraged since the time that Pret a Manger ran out of pomegranate and hibiscus infused water! I take a deep breath and enter the coffee store.

A few minutes later and it's my turn at the counter. A man named Tamás with a gold badge on his jacket that reads "Boutique Coffee Specialist" takes my caffeine filled order. As he does so I'm staring at his badge, wondering why 'boutique'? Is the shop supposed to be 'boutique'? I look around, but the place is anything, but small. Or maybe it's Tamás that's 'boutique'? Are they poking fun at this poor lamb's diminutive stature? The cruel bastards!

I'm now at Brody Studios, clutching my Nespresso bag. Rupert glares at it.

"Bloody yuppie!" he sneers.

I decide to ignore, for the time being, the fact that I'm being called a 'yuppie' by a man named Rupert, although I do make a note of it in my Filofax. A waiter comes over and takes our order. In the background the story telling has begun. A Ukrainian war photographer has just taken to the stage and is telling a story about having to take a shit on the frontline during enemy fire.

"Did you know Jennifer Lawrence has become a regular here?" says Rupert.

"At Brody Studios?" I respond.

"Yeah. In town shooting some film called Red Sparrow apparently."

"Cool!"

The Ukrainian man has finished telling his story. An American girl has now taken to the stage and is telling a story about stuffing a dead dog into a suitcase. To be fair though, I'm not really paying too much attention as I'm too busy scanning the room for Jennifer Lawrence. She may not know it, but she's being hunted. It's like The Hunger Games all over again. My phone buzzes. It's a message from my boutique wife.

"Did you get the Nespresso capsules?" she asks.

"Yes baby." I respond.

"Who's that?" asks Rupert.

"Zsuzsa, asking if I picked up the Nespresso capsules."

Rupert shakes his head.

"What?"

"Bunch of yuppies!" he says.

There he goes again!!

"I'm not a yuppie!" I protest, before adding "I grew up in deepest, darkest Wales! I went to a comprehensive, and..." But then I'm stopped in my tracks as my phone buzzes. It's my boutique wife again.

"Don't be too late honey. Remember that Mila has her first cello lesson tomorrow morning."

Then it hits me. A moment of clarity. I'm a man sitting in a private members club, frequented by Jennifer Lawrence, quaffing continental lager and wine with a friend named Rupert. I also shop at a boutique coffee shop and my nearly nine month old baby is taking cello lessons.

"And what?" asks Rupert.

"Oh, nothing." I say, as we watch a German man tell a story about how he responded to a midlife crisis by opening a trampoline park.

Day 318

The Nightmare!

I'm confused.

We're at a local restaurant grabbing breakfast. Mila has just woken up, and for some unknown reason, appears to hate me. I noticed her buggy moving, went to see if she was okay, smiled at her sleepy little face and received a fearful glare in return.

"Are you okay little lady?" I asked.

She simply glared back.

I unbuttoned her clips and lifted her out of the buggy. Mila screamed. Everyone in the restaurant stared. I handed Mila to Zsuzsa, she became calm and smiley. Zsuzsa handed her back to me, the scream returned. And now we're back to the start of this tale with me being confused.

"What's wrong Mila? It's me! Daddy!"

"Aaaaaaaarrrrrrggghhhh!"

Tears are now pouring down her face. She seems terrified! I glance around at the other diners. Beady eyes everywhere, staring at me over their ham and eggs. They probably think I'm stealing her!

"I'm her Dad!" I want to defiantly state. "Go back to your ham and eggs, peasants! There is no baby snatching going on here!"

everyone else, it's always been a dream of mine to have a little baby girl who can do a mean Al Pacino impression.

Anyway, what the devil is Zsusza on about? Why on earth wouldn't Mila want to master an Al Pacino impression!? I make a mental note to advise Zsuzsa later not to think twice in such a short space of time again.

"Look on the bright side. At least she likes one of us." says Zsuzsa.

The next few hours are spent with Daddy on a full-on charm offensive assault. I take Mila to the swings, I repeatedly kiss her chubby little cheeks, I change her piss filled nappy and I feed her baby slop. Eventually, Mila begins to thaw and appears to stop seeing me as an evil super-villain who punches kittens and murders mummies.

It's the afternoon. To cement my newfound 'good-guy' status I'm reading her a book. It's an English translation of a popular Hungarian book about a couple of friends. One is a snail and the other a ladybird. I find it hard to believe that a snail and a ladybird could ever be great mates given their vastly differing lifestyles, but I decide to bite my tongue and read this preposterous tosh to her anyway, as Mila seems to like it.

"There was Flutter the butterfly, Stanley the stag beetle, Leapy the grasshopper and Bubble the baby beetle." I say.

"Bubble." says Mila.

Zsuzsa and I stare at each other in astonishment.

"Did you hear that?" I ask.

Zsuzsa nods, excitedly.

"Bubble." I say.

"Bubble." says Mila!

"Bubble." says Zsuzsa.

"Bubble." says Mila.

Hooray! Our little baby girl has said her first word on her nine-month birthday! She hasn't got a bloody clue what it means, but that doesn't matter. She said "Bubble!"

"Speaking at nine months! That's early isn't it?" I ask.

"I think so." beams Zsuzsa.

"Maybe she's a genius! Maybe she's the next Einstein?" I suggest.

We both gaze upon our little girl. Mila grabs a toilet roll and attempts to eat it. Zsuzsa tries to wrestle it off her while I begin to scour the net to see if Al Pacino has ever said the word "bubble" on film.

Day 325

Caractacus Hutchins

I'm trying in vain to put a nappy on my baby's naked little arse, when I'm hit by a moment of inspiration. I am suddenly Archimedes sitting in a bath. I am Sir Isaac Newton rubbing his sore head after being hit with an apple. I am Bruce Willis in The Sixth Sense when his wife's wedding ring falls to the ground.

A NAPPY CHANGING MACHINE!

Why does this not already exist? Think about it. How much easier would your life be if you had a simple machine that you could dip a baby in whenever they needed a fresh nappy? Something like a vacuum packing machine that specializes in baby butts. Dip them in, placing their legs in stirrups and voila! Obviously you'd need a baby to feel its full benefit, but still.

People may scoff. People may laugh. People may mock. People no doubt scoffed at Archimedes when he revealed his meat and two veg to the other people sitting in a public bath and shouted "Eureka!". But look at him now! Okay, he's probably a bit on the bony side, but you remember him don't you? People will remember me in the same way. I will be lauded and held up as a bloody hero to millions of shit covered parents while they are dipping their baby in their very own Hutchins machine (obviously it should be named after its creator to cement my legacy). Maybe I could even create a premium one with three different compartments. One to clean, one to cream and one to apply the nappy. Similar to the process of making scotch eggs (where you dip your meaty egg in flour, then egg, then breadcrumbs)!

Later that day I meet up with Zsuzsa in the throbbing heart of Pest. She has Mila strapped to her and she's sleepy. So sleepy in fact, that later this evening she will give Mila a bath and forget to remove her socks.

"What do you think honey?" I ask.

"About what?" she replies.

"Getting my nappy-changing machine patented?"

"Okay."

But there's no conviction in her voice. No passion. I can see right through her and she's not enthused by my nappy-changing idea! I'm perplexed. Does she not recognize real genius when it's smack bang in front of her!? Does she not see me in my true guise? The modern day incarnation of Caractacus Potts? Does she not remember that this is the same man who once put a shelf up in our old flat, and only ruined half of the wall in the process? Where's the confidence?

I'm disappointed. I thought she'd be all over this shit, chomping at the bit to get her hands on such a machine. After all, trying to dress Mila now is akin to putting a bow-tie on an eel. She's a slippery little pickle who refuses to stay still and cooperate. I never realized how easy the whole nappy-changing process was until our little cub decided it was about time to get mobile and start moving around all over the place.

I sigh, but then I look at my beautiful, sleep-deprived wife and I soften. I can't be too harsh on her. She hasn't slept since August! Anyway, I remember that she had a similar, initial response to my design to combine a baby's bottle with a hamster-style feeder, to go on the side of the cot. Four thousand night-time trips to the cot to offer her nipple to a screaming baby later however, and her tune has significantly changed.

[173]

"Will you hurry up and make that bloody hamster-technology inspired baby feeder!" she now says, whilst nursing her savaged nipples.

No, she'll come around. She will be my partner in crime and my biggest supporter. In fact, maybe I'll name it in her honour to show my gratitude to her for being my muse and for all those sleepless nights. As a selfless act I may even forget my initial plan to call it The Hutchins Machine. I'll be like Jesus, who I hear also refused to give his name to a nappy-changing machine.

In years to come, babies' arses all over the word will be covered by…The Zsuzsa. The poor lamb's earned it.

Day 335

The Inconvenient Tooth

I'm sitting in a dentist's chair in the heart of Budapest. A dentist with a thick Hungarian accent, who looks uncannily like the insane, evil surgeon from The Human Centipede is just about to drop a bombshell on me.

"Dead. It is dead." he says nonchalantly.

"Are you sure?" I respond.

"Yes. Your tooth is dead. Pretty sure, I am."

I didn't even realise it was ill.

I'm taken aback by his matter-of-fact tone. He sounds like a heartless, Eastern European Yoda! Where the devil is his bedside manner? Does he not realise how close my tooth and I were? He was one of my favourites! Undoubtedly in my top thirty two! We've spent nearly thirty-five years together since he first tore his way through my infantile, gummy mouth. We've shared so many good times, so many meals out together. So many gastronomic adventures! He was there when I first kissed my wife! Right in the thick of it, the pervy little bastard! Am I just meant to let him go? Just like that?

Hang on a minute. He said "pretty sure". Maybe he's wrong. Maybe he has been wrongly pronounced dead, just like Tom Hanks in the film Castaway?

"Only pretty sure?" I ask.

At this, the dentist picks up the liquid nitrogen drenched piece of cotton wool that he was only moments earlier applying to my sadly deceased tooth with tweezers, and presses it against one of my other teeth.

"Aaaaaarrrrggghh!" I respond. The pain is excruciating!

"If still living it was, the same pain you would have felt."

Fuck you Yoda!

"So what now?" I ask nervously.

"Now holes I will drill into the tooth, treat the root with tiny needles and then next week we will meet for a new tooth."

He wanders off and returns a few seconds later holding a drill. He holds the drill ominously, leans over me and peers at me over the top of his glasses. He smiles.

"Now, I will drill you. If pain you will feel, raise your hand."

Fear is rising. What if this is all a horrible mistake? What if my tooth isn't completely dead? What if it's just in a coma? What if it wakes up just as this animal is about to drill into its living nerve?

The dentist thinks for a moment.

"Although to be fair, you won't actually need to raise your arm if you feel pain. Scream you will! Agony it will be!"

Wonderful stuff.

I hear the whirr of the drill and I am afraid.

The drill connects with my tooth and the process begins.

"There is a film. An old film. A film with Dustin Hoffman." The dentist says over the excruciating sound of the drill boring into my poor tooth. "The name, I don't remember. But there is tooth drilling with no pain killer. Excellent way to get information!"

Er…

The drilling stops.

"Using a series of tiny needles I will now treat your tooth." he proudly claims.

I decide that I need to climb into my 'mind-bungalow', which is very similar to Sherlock Holmes' 'mind-palace', but more homely and without so many levels. I clamber in and begin to write a short script in my head. It's a about a police officer named Tim who's on a raid with his partner, Steve Guttenberg (star of Police Academy, Cocoon and Three Men and a Baby). In this script Steve Guttenberg is playing himself. They're chatting in a police car about the breakdown of Tim's marriage. Then they're entering a drug den in an attempt to apprehend drug lords. A shoot-out ensues and the baddies are shot. Suddenly other police officers arrive and arrest Tim and Steve. We discover that Steve Guttenberg is imaginary, the shot people aren't drug lords and that Tim is simply a civilian having a mental episode following his divorce. Tim gets sent to prison, but he doesn't mind, because as luck would have it, he's put in the same room as his dear friend and hero, Steve Guttenberg.

The dentist puts his tiny needles away. He's finished. I'm thinking about my script idea and wondering if he's sneakily slipped me any psychedelic drugs.

"Next week, same time?" he asks.

I nod sadly and head home to organise a memorial for my beloved tooth (RIP). I will give him the sea (aka wine) burial he always dreamt of.

Day 340
Trainspotting

We're spending the afternoon having a delightful family trip on a railway train run by slave children.

"Honey. What the hell are you writing?" says Zsuzsa who has just appeared over my shoulder and is reading what I'm writing.

"I'm just writing about our trip on the train run by slave children." I say.

"We've been over this! They aren't slave children, honey!"

"Are they children?"

"Yes."

"Do they get paid?"

"No."

"Then surely they're slave children?"

"They're volunteers! They can leave if they want!" Zsuzsa protests, before adding "You're still writing this down aren't you!? Why are you writing this down? Stop it! This isn't court!"

So anyway, we're spending the afternoon travelling on a railway run by child volunteers (aka slave children). I first became aware of the peculiar child-railway phenomenon when watching a programme about Budapest on Channel 4, and then soon after discovering that it was basically next door to our flat. It sounded freaky, so naturally I harangued Zsuzsa into agreeing to visit it. Eventually the haranguing worked.

As an aside, 'harangued'! Great word isn't it? I make a mental note to do more haranguing so that I can use it more often.

We arrive at a railway station in the Buda Hills. Mila has just fallen asleep and Zsuzsa asks me to go and buy the train tickets. I enter the railway station and stand at the counter. I then notice a tiny boy, maybe twelve years old, peering over the counter.

"Halo (Hello)" he says.

"Halo. Kettö jegyet köszönöm (Hello. Two tickets please?)" I reply, like a bloody native.

He stares at me.

"Bocsánat (sorry)?" he says.

Simpleton, obviously.

"Uh…kettö jegyet köszönöm?" I repeat.

He just stares at me blankly. Another child approaches. Another boy. Maybe fourteen years old.

"Halo." he says

"Halo." I say. "Kettö jegyet köszönöm."

He frowns.

"Angol (English)?" he says.

"Igen (yes)" I reply.

"What would you like?" he then asks, switching to perfect English.

"Uh…two tickets please?"

He nods knowingly, turns to the twelve year old and says "Kettö jegyet."

Hold on! What are these infantile clowns up to? That's clearly, exactly what I've been saying all along!

A few minutes later and we're on the train.

"I just don't get it." I say. "Kettö jegyet köszönöm! What's wrong with that? Why didn't they understand me?"

"I understand you." says Zsuzsa reassuringly. "But then again I think I understand you in the same way that a mother understands their mumbling toddler" she adds, a little less reassuringly. "If you'd emphasised the 't' I'm sure they would have understood you. Ketttttttttttö"

She sounds as though she has a stammer.

A tiny little girl in a hat is approaching us to check our tickets. I look at her and can't help but chuckle.

"I don't even know why we bothered buying tickets." I say. "I reckon I could take these children if they tried to kick us off for not having a ticket. Probably all of them, or at least ten at once."

Zsuzsa rolls her eyes, pretending not to be impressed that I could defeat a bunch of small children at wrestling.

"Also, I've been thinking." I say. "I've decided that the owners of this railway might actually be geniuses! Think about it! Employ a bunch of kids, you don't have to pay them as they're too young to legally be paid, AND, they get twice as many customers because of the kids! I mean, people are curious! I wouldn't have been bothered about coming here if it was just a bog standard train run by a group of grumpy, middle aged men."

"I don't think that's the point." says Zsuzsa. "I think they're scouts (aka slaves) and it's an honour for them."

At least I think that's what she says, but the truth is, I'm not listening. My mind is alight.

"I'm amazed there aren't more businesses following this model! Imagine it! A hotel run by children! Or shops run by children! Or prisons!"

But now Zsuzsa is the one who doesn't seem to be listening, but it's not a problem. Let her enjoy the child slave railway with our little baby today. She deserves it. They both do. Anyway, she'll listen soon enough. She'll listen when I'm rolling in money from my billion pound prison empire run by little children, you mark my words.

Day 347
Easy Riders, Raging Baby

FRIDAY

We've just arrived at a lake on the Hungarian/Austria border that quite magnificently translates as Lake Cesspit. The in-laws are with us and the plan is to hire three bikes between the five of us (the five includes baby Mila), and then spend the next three days making our way around the lake. We hire the bikes and off we go, looking uncannily like an alternate reality Goonies. Zsuzsa has elected to drive today so it's just me, the in-laws and a baby.

The scenery is spectacular and as I wend my merry way through the Austrian countryside I can't help but feel like I'm in the film Easy Rider. I'm playing Peter Fonda and naturally, Mila is Dennis Hopper. You don't need me to tell you that the mother in law is obviously Jack Nicholson.

SATURDAY

We're staying in a lovely little rustic motel/vineyard just over the Hungarian border. It's three in the morning and Mila is wailing like a banshee. Alas, it's my turn to deal with her and Zsuzsa's turn to pretend to be asleep. With Mila screaming as though she were on fire, I decide to change her nappy. I put her down on the spare bed, turn on my phone torch, remove her nappy and then fumble around in a vain attempt to put a fresh nappy on her pink little butt. Mila is refusing to play ball and is howling and rolling around on the bed like a South American footballer following a rogue gust of wind. I'm exasperated. I'm tired. I'm also naked by the way. Suddenly the door to the hotel room opens and in walks the mother-in-law to help calm my distressed baby. Did I mention I was naked? I'm also surprised as I thought our door was locked. The mother-in-law sees me and continues with her relentless advance. What the devil is she doing!? I then notice that she doesn't have her glasses on and is yet to realise that the only thing I'm wearing is a look of utter despair. I do the only thing that I can do and dive for cover behind the bed. Luckily, Zsuzsa intervenes and shepherds her mother out of the room like a trusty old sheep dog.

It's now the following morning. It's my turn to drive and we've agreed to regroup in an hour or so in the next village. Mila is fast asleep in the back of the car as we approach the Austrian border. I notice border police stopping cars and get a familiar feeling. It's the same feeling that I get every time I walk through the "Nothing to Declare" section at airports. Namely, the feeling that I am coming across like a heroin smuggler. Every time, I try and appear as un-heroin-smuggler-like as possible, but in my head I'm exuding heroin-smuggler-ness. Now, as I approach the border police, I'm trying desperately to not look like a child snatcher! I pull to a stop and the border policeman's mirror tinted face glares in. I smile at him, probably in the exact style of a child snatcher. He waves me through and I breathe a sigh of relief.

Twenty minutes later and I've reached a village called Rust, parked in a street called Seekanal and I'm awaiting the cyclists' arrival. At least I hope that's the street name rather than some kind of designated activity area. After a full day of cycling yesterday, I'm a little sore, and that's pretty much the last thing I'm seeking right now if truth be told.

SUNDAY

The final leg of our cycling adventure. We spent last night in a spa/hotel and we're now sitting in a lovely little pop-up cafe/bar in the middle of a vineyard. The temperature is in the mid-thirties so we've found a little shade, to cool ourselves while we quench our thirst with white wine spritzer.

"Mila had five poohs today!" Zsuzsa proudly announces. "Two before breakfast! Just like her Daddy!"

Naturally both Mila and I are furious with her mother's loose tongue. I'm internally debating how to deal with her, when Mila takes the bull by the horns. She reaches out, grabs her mother's drink and pours it away. Unfortunately for me the majority goes over my crotch. My hands and my clothes are drenched. I sigh and then turn to face the sun in an attempt to dry off. Out of the corner of my eye I notice the father-in-law watching me. I turn to him and he smiles.

"Foreskin." he says.

"Uh." I reply.

"White wine. Good for skin."

"Oh. Is it?" I say.

I have to admit, I'm a little relived.

A few hours later and our cycling adventure is over. We're all tired and sore, and as we head back to Budapest I'm remembering when I used to (try) to play the guitar. After a while the skin on the tips of my fingers became hard and tough to deal with the constant strumming. As I nurse my sore bottom I can't help but wonder if cyclists experience a similar phenomenon. I mean, do all professional cyclists have very tough butt skin? Don't pretend that it's something that you've never pondered.

Day 355
Shopping for Fleas

I'm sitting in my office, drenched in baby piss. I'm trying my best to style it out, trying to convince myself that this isn't baby piss. It's not! It's a new aftershave from Dolce & Gabbana. The hottest fragrance in town. The kind of thing that Matthew McConaughey would promote, whilst some young, Brazilian super-model drapes her limbs all over him. A vibrant new eau de toilette.

Nah.

Who am I trying to kid. It's baby piss.

Why am I sitting in my office covered in baby piss? Well, obviously my baby pissed on me, but let's go back in time a bit so that I can storify the shit out of my urine-drenched tale. So come on you! Jump in my DeLorean and fasten your seatbelt! We're going back in time. Back to a time when shirts were dry as a bone. The magical time of just over one hour ago.

JUST OVER ONE HOUR AGO...

My shirt is lovely and dry and I'm with my beloved wife and our fleshy little heir to the Hutchins/Ferencz fortune. We're on the hunt for furniture to furnish a new flat that we've just bought. Our brand spanking new purchase is a lovely little place in Budapest that we are planning on AirBnB-ing the absolute living daylights out of. We've been looking for a place to buy for about a year or so now and

I'm delighted that we've finally found one. Mainly because it means that I no longer need to walk around buildings tapping walls and looking thoughtful (a trick that I've picked up from watching Location, Location, Location) in an attempt to appear as though I vaguely know what I'm doing.

Anyway, we've just arrived at Esceri flea market, a remarkable gem full of antique furniture, communist memorabilia, Eastern European treasures, beautiful finds and also copious amounts of worthless tat. Bargains are here to be had, as are absolute, unashamed fleecings. As such I'm about to be forbidden from speaking.

"Why is it called a flea market?" I say as we stroll towards the market epicentre." I mean, they don't sell fleas do they?"

"I don't know honey." replies Zsuzsa.

"Maybe they used to sell fleas at one time?"

"I don't think so honey. Anyway, stop speaking now."

"What? Why?"

"Because as soon as the sellers hear your British voice they'll quadruple the price of everything!"

And so we begin wandering through the forests of chairs, tables, lamps, typewriters, pictures, gramophones, cameras and pots. Just a Hungarian lady and her mute companion with a baby strapped to his front. Zsuzsa is rummaging through old stuff while I'm Googling why 'flea markets' are called 'flea markets' (originated from a market in Paris that specialised in shabby second-hand goods that looked as though they might contain fleas if you must know).

I'm snapped from my mobile screen by someone speaking to me. I look up.

"Jó napot! (Good day!)" says a moustache that I think has a little bit of man behind it.

I look at Zsuzsa nervously, not knowing how to respond. Obviously under normal circumstances I would launch into an impressive monologue of perfect Hungarian, but today I've been forbidden. Today I must play mute or risk the success of our treasure-finding mission.

"Jó napot!" replies Zsuzsa for both of us, whilst motioning for me to make myself scarce. I oblige and move on with pace.

This routine continues for the next thirty minutes. On one occasion I drop my guard and mutter a phrase of English which is immediately pounced upon by a gypsy lady seller. Thankfully though, Zsuzsa is on hand to fix the situation by telling the gypsy lady seller that I'm a very, very poor man from a mining community in Wales. They seem to buy it, and feeling sorry for Zsuzsa's poor choice of husband, even grant her good luck!

"If a gypsy wishes you good luck, it's a very, very lucky thing indeed!" beams Zsuzsa.

Forty odd minutes later, and laden with an old suitcase and a couple of paintings, we're back in the car, pointed in the direction of my office. Something is troubling me.

"I can't believe she pissed on me!" I say.

"Honey. It's baby piss! It doesn't smell! Being pissed on by a baby is the best possible scenario!" says Zsuzsa, trying to placate me.

"Bullshit! Not being pissed on is the best scenario. Followed by Mila pissing on *you*, then comes Mila pissing on me, and then finally a stranger pissing on me."

We drive on in silence. Something then occurs to me.

"You know Airbnb?" I say.

"Yes." replies Zsuzsa.

"Why is it bnb? I mean, Airbnbs don't provide breakfast."

Zsuzsa thinks for a moment.

"I don't know." she says, before adding "To be honest I've also never known what the 'Air' bit is about either."

Goddamnit! She's got a point!

"Maybe they should just be called 'B'?" I suggest.

"But maybe B.com had already been taken." says Zsuzsa, like the wise old owl that she is.

I park the car.

"I can't believe I'm covered in baby piss!! It's all over my shirt!" I moan.

"Don't worry honey." says Zsuzsa. "It'll dry in no time."

"But I've got a video call with the CMO of one of Europe's biggest companies in a matter of minutes! I'M COVERED IN BABY PISS!"

And now we're back at the beginning of this yarn. I'm about to begin a video call with a big cheese. I'm worried as I don't think the piss-drenched look is overly professional. After all, this is not Scotland. The video call starts buzzing. It's him! La Grande Fromage! Think Gareth! Think! What are you going to do!? What would Batman do!?

"Hi! Gareth here! Do you mind if we just do an audio call today? Few technical problems at this end. I can't seem to get this camera to work."

Good old Batman.

Day 364

Gareth vs The Post Office

"Hello sir. I'm afraid you need to put the country on the envelope." says the lady behind the counter of the central Budapest post office that I'm currently standing in.

"But I have. '*Wales*'." I say.

She stares at me blankly.

"No. We need the country."

"Wales. It is a country. It's written there on the envelope." I say, pointing.

She is perplexed. She turns to a man sitting at the counter next to her and launches into rapid burst of advanced Hungarian. The man stands up and addresses me.

"Sir. We need the country on the envelope."

I'm starting to wonder if I'm dead.

"It's on there." I say.

"Where? I don't see it." he replies.

"Right here. Wales."

The man sighs.

"But we need the country."

"Wales is a country!"

"I don't think so sir."

"It is! I grew up there!"

"No. I don't think it's a country. I think it's a region."

"What!? It's a country! It's in the UK!"

"Oh! It's in the UK?"

"Yes!"

"Then please put England on the envelope."

"No! It's not in England! It's the country of Wales!"

The man and the woman look at each other and then speak to each other softly and inaudibly. The woman behind the counter holds up the envelope and studies it. A man around thirty years of age, standing in the queue behind me, has been listening to our conversation with interest. He steps forward.

"Excuse me." he says. "But I don't think Wales is a country."

I turn and stare at him, agog. This is the most agog that I have been in a long time.

"What?" I say.

"The Olympics. There's no Wales team in The Olympics. It's Great Britain. The country is Great Britain."

He smiles. It's the self-satisfied smile of a buffoon. The man and woman behind the counter nod in agreement at the buffoon. I need to put an end to this madness.

"There's a Wales football team. There's a Wales rugby team! Tom Jones, Ryan Giggs, Gareth Bale, Catherine Zeta Jones, Christian Bale, Anthony Hopkins, Super Ted, Pingu...Ruth Madoc! All Welsh! Believe me, Wales is a country. I should know. I'm half Welsh and grew up there! It's a country and it's written on the envelope! Right there!"

Boom! How do you like those apples?

Silence follows. They are no doubt in awe of my impassioned and impressive monologue. Eventually, the woman plucks up the courage to speak.

"Who's Ruth Madoc?" she says.

"It doesn't matter!" I defiantly declare.

"I think Christian Bale is actually American." says the random man in the queue.

I glare at him. It is a powerful glare. A fearsome glare. He visibly withers and his testicles no doubt shrink. He slinks back into the shadows and back under the rock from whence he came, vanquished. I turn to the man and lady behind the counter. I'm exuding an almighty, dominant aura. They feel it instantly the man nods to the woman and promptly returns to his duties. I make eye contact with the woman. The poor lamb has received one hell of a public beating today, but on the flip side she has learnt a valuable life lesson. She picks up my envelope. She reaches for a pen.

She crosses out Wales and writes GB.

"Következő! (Next!)"

Day 370
The Wild Child

It's a lovely sunny evening in Budapest and I've just arrived at a delightful restaurant. Zsuzsa, Mila and a couple of friends are already here, tucking into unidentifiable meat and fröccs (wine spritzer).

"Hello!" I say cheerfully.

Zsuzsa looks at me with the same expression as a dog once did in Battersea Dog's Home.

"Please take her honey. She's worn me out. I've got nothing left. I'm done." she says, a broken woman.

She holds Mila out towards me. Mila squeals with delight, her eyes vibrant and wild. I nod and collect my little baby girl in my arms. She screams with joy and starts jigging up and down.

"She's been like it all day." says Zsuzsa. "She's got so much energy! I don't understand it!"

Mila grins at me and bounces up and down some more. I have to admit, she is acting uncannily like Kris Akabusi today. If she could talk she would undoubtedly be bellowing "Awooga!" at this moment.

I order a wienerschitzel and the four of us chat while I attempt to restrain our little wild child.

A waiter approaches with my wienerschnitzel. He has his back to us while he carefully places the dish in front of me.

Then it happened.

Out of the corner of my eye I notice a chubby little baby arm reach out and pinch the waiter's arse. Mila retracts her arm quickly and suddenly morphs into a quiet, chilled-out, perfectly behaved baby. The waiter spins around and glares at me. I know that glare! I've seen it before! It's an incriminating glare!

It's 1980 and I'm on a sunny-ish beach in West Wales. The beach is in a place called Porthmadog and I'm with my father and my brother (I can't remember where my mother was at this moment). I'm about four and my brother is one and a bit. The three of us are sitting in a row and if memory serves me correctly my father is wearing hideous, brown swimming trunks (that's not relevant to the story, but still, he should be ashamed). A young woman wanders past in a bikini. My brother, Ross, chooses this moment to let out the loudest wolf whistle that any baby, anywhere in the world has ever produced. I have vivid memories of the young woman glaring at my father. It was an incriminating glare. She then burst into a furious tirade, shouting whilst jabbing an angry finger in his direction.

"It was the baby." I remember him saying while pointing to this tiny little baby boy.

She was having none of it.

It's now 2017 and we're back in the Hungarian restaurant. I'm being glared at.

"It was the baby." I say.

The waiter just gives me a withering look and wanders off

shaking his head. I'm aghast. I turn to Zsuzsa.

"Mila just pinched that waiter's arse and I think he thinks it was me!" I say.

"That's nice honey." replies Zsuzsa.

"What!? No it's not nice! Please tell the waiter when he comes over. Please tell him it was Mila. Please tell him that I didn't pinch his arse!"

Zsuzsa looks at me and I can instantly see that her mind is somewhere else. About five seconds of silence follows, before Zsuzsa speaks.

"I think Mila might be a bit like an Arab." she says.

"What?"

"Well she seems to love drinking hot tea in hot weather."

"What?"

I look at my tired wife and accept defeat. She has been temporarily broken by our little wild baby. She appears to be malfunctioning. I decide to drop it and accept that the waiter will always think of me as some kind of British, Donald Trump-esque deviant. But that's fine.

We just can never, ever come here ever again.

Day 379
Knickers!

We're driving to Mila's weekly swimming lesson and as usual, we're late. As a result I'm weaving through the Budapest traffic like Herbie the Love Bug.

"Slow down honey!" pleads Zsuzsa.

I glance at the sat nav. Our estimated arrival time is 10:31. That's one minute late! This simply will not do. Not on my watch!

"I'm fine honey. I'm driving perfectly safely." I reply.

It's true. I am driving perfectly safely, but unbeknownst to Zsuzsa, I'm also racing the sat nav. This is a classic case of man vs machine. This is Rocky vs Ivan Drago. This is Sarah Conner taking down The Terminator. This is Garry Kasparov battling it out with Deep Blue in a brutal game of action chess.

"Honey!"

"Okay, okay, okay."

I apply the brakes, but just enough that I'm only going one or two miles an hour over the speed limit. I think I can still whittle a precious minute off our journey, defeat this soulless electronic son of a bitch and laugh in its LCD face.

Mila decides to chime in.

"Kaki!"

Oh yes. Mila has started to call me Daddy. The only issue is that it often sounds more like "Kaki" which is Hungarian for 'pooh'. Basically she calls me 'Pooh'. I'm hoping it doesn't stick.

We pull up at the sports centre. It's 10:32. I'm disappointed, but equally determined. You may have won the battle sat nav, but mark my words, you will not win the war! I will have my sweet revenge when you least expect it. I will serve it cold and embarrass you in front of your electronic peers. You just wait.

"Bring Mila in. I'll go and pay!" barks Zsuzsa as she darts out of the car and across the car park like a speedy Hungarian corgi in full flight.

I move to the back seat, pick Mila up and carry her inside the leisure centre.

"Kaki!"

I meet Zsuzsa at the entrance to the pool. She is already in her swimming costume and I hand her our baby daughter. But I can tell instantly something is wrong.

"Honey, I forgot my knickers!" she says.

"Oh. Okay." I say and shrug. I mean what can I do?

"They're in the glove box. Can you go and fetch them for me and hide them somewhere in the ladies changing room while we're swimming?"

Wait…what?

Before I can respond, Zsuzsa runs off to the pool with Mila. I stand there for a moment and process what she's just asked. I play the scene out in my head.

I imagine myself approaching the ladies changing room clutching a pair of ladies knickers. I put my ear to the door and listen for any sounds. All seems quiet so I slowly open the door. I look around. Empty. Still clutching the knickers I sneak into the changing room in the style of a cartoon character. I'm about to place the knickers into a shadowy corner when I hear footsteps. I spin around and our eyes meet. It's a naked old lady. Her face is a picture of fear and rage. She shouts at me in Hungarian. I mumble in a vain attempt to explain myself, but the Hungarian for "I'm not a pervert. I'm just hiding my wife's knickers in a dark corner." escapes me. The door barges open and a burly security guard stands there. He glowers at me. I hold my hands up, but it just looks as though I'm waving ladies knickers in the air. It looks as though I'm bragging! He pounces, twisting my arm behind my back. Before I know what's happening I'm shepherded into a dingy room and the door is locked. I'm held captive until the police arrive. I'm charged with being a sex pest and sentenced to imprisonment in a remote part of Hungary near the Ukrainian border. I'm left to rot, floundering in my own kaki.

I decide that there are worse things in life than wet bikini bottoms.

Day 389

A Lust for Life

It's the day before my forty-first birthday, and like all true heroes, I'm spending it in IKEA buying a selection of delightful cushions.

A year ago to the day, the magnificently named Dr Pop had told us that a tiny, naked human could emerge from my wife's nether regions at any given moment. As I was on driving duties, and also because witnessing the birth of my first child with a raging hang-over didn't sound all that groovy, I'd had a fairly chilled out, civilised fortieth birthday.

"We'll celebrate my fortieth next year yeah?"

"That's a good idea honey!"

"Yeah! It'll be mental!"

But now here I am, surrounded by cushions and saucepans and holding something peculiar called a salad spinner. I console myself by imagining that this is exactly how someone like Iggy Pop would have spent his birthdays. In Hungarian IKEAs. He'd probably have been walking around the store in see-thru clingfilm trousers, but he'd have been carrying a salad spinner, no doubt.

My journey through IKEA on my birthday eve is a solo journey, but it's not a lonely one. Largely because Zsuzsa is guiding me through the store via the magic of FaceTime.

"Now go to the storage zone and buy four rattan baskets! Quickly! The store closes in 5 minutes!"

As I hurtle through the store I can't help but feel as though I'm in a budget version of The Crystal Maze, probably broadcast on Channel 5.

"Honey!" squeaks Zsuzsa through my mobile phone screen as I'm rummaging around, knee deep in wicker. "Don't you think this is such an efficient way to do IKEA!?"

I decide to bite my tongue. and smile sweetly.

It's now the morning after my birthday eve.

"Happy birthday honey!" beams my boutique wife, and hands me a piece of paper with the number '1' written on it.

I stare at the piece of paper with blurry eyes.

"We're having a Numbers-Party-themed birthday!" says Zsuzsa with a spring in her step, whilst punching the air triumphantly like Rocky Balboa.

As I'm sure you're all aware, The Numbers Party is Mila's favourite TV show on her favourite channel, Baby TV. Again, I'm confident that Iggy Pop has had many a Numbers-Party-themed birthday in his time.

I turn the paper and see "Tojas" written on the other side. I know this word. "Eggs!" Sure enough, the paper is prophetic and eggs are shortly consumed.

Throughout the day I'm handed several numbered pieces of

paper, which in turn lead to fun and frolics. For instance, shortly after breakfast, I'm greased up by a tiny Thai lady who then proceeds to clamber all over my egg-filled body. An hour or two later and we're on a guided river cruise down the Danube where an insane audio guide enlightens me with the fact that "Two thirds of the rivers in Hungary are water. The other third is fish." In the afternoon we ride Segways through the streets of Budapest.

As the sun begins to set I'm given a birthday cake with the world "Kaki" (Hungarian for Pooh, and Mila's latest nickname for me) written on it in brown icing. And last, but not least, I'm surprised with a trip to a funky little restaurant.

As we head home to our cushion-strewn, Hungarian love-creche at the end of the evening, I'm exhausted and struggling to hold up my heavy eyelids, but I'm deliriously happy.

I came to Budapest as a childless 39-year-old with a penchant for getting himself into ridiculous situations. A year later and I'm now a 41-year-old Dad with a penchant for getting himself into ridiculous situations. I now have bigger bags under my eyes than ever and more grey hairs than I did before. I fall asleep on the sofa in front of the TV most evenings. I believe that free time is an urban myth and I sometimes pretend that I need to go to the toilet so that I can seek sanctuary in the only sacred solitude that I now have.

As I'm writing this, my beautiful, knackered little Zsuzsa is passed out in a heap on the sofa and I don't think I'm far behind her. Life has certainly changed dramatically in a year, that's for sure. Once there were two, now there are three, and I'd be lying if I said that I didn't miss the happy-go-lucky, carefree life we once had from time to time. It was a riot and I loved it, but would I ever go back to it if offered the choice? Of course not (although ask me again at 05:00 in the morning when my eardrums are being pounded by the sound of baby screams and Zsuzsa is pleading with me to change Mila's shitty nappy).

You know what? Life may have changed beyond all recognition, but (after we've drunk exceptionally potent coffee) our lust for life has never been stronger.

Day 394
Croatia Episode 1 - The Search for Hvar

We're going on a road trip to Croatia and I'm tremendously excited. I love a good road trip.

"It'll be amazing! We'll be like Johnny Depp and Benicio del Toro in 'Fear and Loathing in Las Vegas'! Just you, me and the open road, charging head-first into an adventure!" I say.

"And Mila." adds Zsuzsa.

"Just you, me, a baby and the open road, charging head-first into an adventure!"

"And my parents."

"Er...Just you, me, a baby, the in-laws and the open road, er...charging head-first into an adventure."

I'm trying to remember the film 'Fear and Loathing in Las Vegas'. I remember an open topped car, the desert and debaucerous high-jinx. I can't remember if Johnny Depp or Benicio del Toro brought any parents with them. I decide that they must have.

The first stop of our Croatian adventure is the island of Hvar, which depending on who you speak to is either pronounced Ha-var, Wah or Gshxkbkgyshbkgydjughhb-ar. We load up the car with everything we've ever owned and depart Budapest at about 06:30. According to Google we should arrive in Split in about $7^1/_2$ hours. We then need to catch a 2 hour ferry to Hvar. I'm sharing the driving with my father-in-law.

About 4 hours in and Zsuzsa and her mother are singing nursery rhymes to calm our excitable spawn. I'm taking a breather in the passenger seat while my father-in-law drives. Zsuzsa suddenly hands me some biscuits.

"Honey. Feed my father please."

I decide that I'm up to this challenge, take the biscuits and offer them to my father-in-law.

"No honey! Not to his hand! Into his mouth!"

"Er...what?"

"He needs both hands free to drive! He's tired!"

"But..."

"Honey! Please!"

I reluctantly comply and begin feeding biscuits into my father-in-law's mouth, the bristles of his bushy moustache brushing against my fingers as I do so. I definitely don't remember this bit happening in 'Fear and Loathing in Las Vegas'.

A few hours later and we're approaching Split. I'm now driving, Mila is asleep and 'Joyride' by Roxette is playing via the radio. Party time. Zsuzsa then says something to her father and seconds later I discover a biscuit being stuffed into my mouth. This is madness and highly peculiar behaviour, but I'm on holiday so I roll with it.

At 19:00 hours we arrive on Hvar. It's beautiful, with rugged coastlines surrounding spectacular green mountains, and the sounds of waves crashing and cicadas chanting all around. It's like a live performance of the 'white noise' app that we sometimes use to get Mila to sleep.

Day one is all about exploring. On day two we find a stunning little beach and set up a base camp for a full day of hard-core, extreme baby-beaching.

"It's amazing isn't it?" I say to Zsuzsa.

"Yes, but the sea smells really fishy." she replies, whilst sniffing the air suspiciously.

I make a mental note to drive the fish from the sea, although it'll have to wait until after I've tidied my wardrobe.

Later that evening we return to our apartment and begin unpacking the endless array of bags that we take to the beach now that we have Mila. Zsuzsa reaches inside one bag that has a melon emblazoned on the side, removes a saucy pair of white, satin hot pants and frowns. She's frowning because they are not hers. Still holding the hot pants aloft, she turns towards her mother.

"Anya? (Mum?)"

Her mother looks at the hot pants and shakes her head. Zsuzsa turns towards her father.

"Apa? (Dad?)"

He also shakes his head. They obviously aren't his. They're not his colour.

It's only then that we realise that we have two beach bags with melons emblazoned upon their front. This is strange as this morning we only had one. Slowly it dawns upon us that we have accidentally stolen a random family's clothes.

So, if you happened to be in Jelsa and stumbled across an entire family driving home from the beach, wearing nothing but furious expressions, please tell them we have their clothes.

Next stop, Brela.

To be continued...

Day 399

Croatia Episode II - The Beach

Previously, on The Buda Nest...

We travelled to Hvar from Budapest whilst being force-fed biscuits. The island was beautiful, but the sea was fishy. We stole a random family's clothes and then fled the island with our next destination being Brela...

The first I heard of the beach was in Brela, on the Frankopanska Road.

"We found it yesterday. It's an idyllic, isolated beach on an untouched peninsula." says Mr Tomato.

Mr and Mrs Tomato are friends of ours from Budapest who, like a pair of juicy, ripe stalkers, just happen to be staying in Brela, in the same apartment building as us, at the same time as us! And as much as I'd love their real names to be Mr and Mrs Tomato and for them to be real-life, children's book characters, these are actually their nicknames. The beach that Mr Tomato is referring to is in response to our glum faces on the discovery that all of the beaches in Brela appear to be pebbly.

"I just don't understand it." I say whilst searching through Google. "Look! All of these sites talk about the gorgeous sandy beaches of Brela!"

"I know!" agrees Mr Tomato. "That's why we came to Brela as well (that and to stalk us). But it seems to me that Croatians have a different understanding of sand! You should seriously check out this beach that we found though. It's heavenly! No tiny pebbles!"

The next morning we mentally prepare ourselves to tackle the pebbly beaches of Brela with baby Mila.

"Maybe it'll be alright." I say to Zsuzsa. "Maybe Mila will enjoy the pebbles."

"Honey. Mila will try and eat the pebbles. She will find them inexplicably delicious." she replies.

"Maybe she won't. Maybe you're underestimating her intelligence. Maybe she's smarter than you give her credit for! She's not stupid you know?"

Half an hour later, and having grown tired of screaming "No!" and grabbing pebbles from Mila's mouth after she attempted to eat the entire beach in a pebble-eating frenzy, we leave the beach. We join Mr & Mrs Tomato and together travel in a convoy to this sacred, secluded paradise. Mr Tomato is, of course, leading the convoy as only he knows the secret path to the secret beach.

Twenty minutes later and Mr Tomato leads us off the main road into a busy secret car-park. We get out of our cars.

"The secret beach is this way." says an enthusiastic Mr Tomato, pointing in the direction of a row of beach front shops selling Croatia hats, mugs and flags.

We follow Mr Tomato past the busy secret shops, via several busy secret beach-front bars, meandering our way through the hoards and throngs of sweaty beach-dwellers who must have heard about this secret paradise via hushed whispers in secret corners of Brela. A few minutes later and we arrive at 'The Beach'. True to his word there are no bite-sized pebbles for Mila to munch on. Instead the ground is covered in fist sized, jagged rocks. Hmmm.

We hurl our pop-up tent next to a jet ski rental hut. The sun is beating down on us and there's a severe lack of shade on the beach/quarry but I'm determined to make the most of it. I pop my snorkel on and head to the water. Mr Tomato sees me, shakes his head and then points to my feet.

"Make sure you wear shoes in the water. It's full of hedgehogs!" he says.

"Huh?" I reply.

"Hedgehogs! Sea hedgehogs!"

"Er…"

"Those spikey ball things!"

I'm wondering if Mr Tomato is suffering from sun-stroke, but pop the snorkel on and stick my face under the water to humour him. Sea urchins. Super sharp, super spikey sea urchins as far as the eye can see. Sea urchins looking for a lovely human shaped pin cushion to house their many pins. I resurface.

"So let me get this straight." I say. "We're at this secret, idyllic beach, surrounded by beach dwellers, next to a jet ski rental hut, precariously perched on a bed of jagged rocks, melting in the sun without shade and we can't walk in the water without puncturing our feet on a…er…sea hedgehog?"

"Yes. We like it." replies Mr Tomato.

I make a mental note never to accept a beach recommendation from a man named after a fruit or vegetable again, and return to my baking hot tent on the jagged rocks. I sit down in the sweltering heat and turn to by beautiful wife. She returns my gaze, and smiles sweetly. Suddenly I feel contented. She leans in, to whisper sweet nothings into my ear.

"Honey. I think Mila's done a massive poop. It's your turn to change her." she softly says.

Oh, my beautiful holiday paradise.

Day 414

Our Little One Year Old

August 2nd

I'm sitting in a Burger King car-park, in Budapest, at 01:00 in the morning.

I'm not dogging, and I'm not a burger fiend or anything like that (well, no more than any other sane person). No, my brother and his tiny family are coming to stay and I'm lying in wait near the airport to collect them. Just to clarify, by 'tiny family', I don't mean that they are a family of primordial dwarfs. More that he's bringing his little children with him as well as his beloved wife. One is a few days shy of 7, and the other is 3. I'm excited about seeing them, but also bracing myself. With three children together in a confined environment, naturally, there's a storm coming. Hurricane Hutchins is almost upon us.

August 4th

Today is exactly one year since our little lady burst her way into this world via my beautiful wife's groin. I can't believe it's been a year! A year since a doctor muttered the immortal words, "Come! You can see the head!" I can still hear the sound of Zsuzsa's primal scream drowning out the operatic tones of Pavarotti's Nessun Dorma! I can still feel the strange feeling that I felt when I was handed a little purple baby while a Hungarian doctor babbled away to me in incomprehensible Hungarian. I still remember driving home from the hospital on my own in the evening (Zsuzsa and Mila needed to stay in for a few days) and plonking myself down on the sofa with a bottle of red. I can't believe that it's 21 months since Zsuzsa muttered the words, "Honey, can you see a cross here?"

It seems like only yesterday that we were a care-free, happy-go-lucky couple who would swan off to far-flung corners of the world at the drop of a hat. A couple who got their fair share of sleep and could spend a rainy Sunday snoozing on the sofa or binge-watching entire seasons of House of Cards, should we choose. That life has now been put on hold for the next 18 years or so.

We celebrate our little lady's first birthday at a stunning winery/restaurant near Lake Balaton with family and friends. Mila seems to be overjoyed. A great day to finish off a quite extraordinarily wonderful year.

August 7th

Today Mila took it upon herself to start calling her Uncle Ross, 'Blub'. Uncle Blub. It's got a nice ring to it. Uncle Blub claimed not to take it personally, but I did notice him sucking in his gut around Mila for the rest of the day.

August 9th

Today Uncle Blub and his family are departing Hungary and heading back to a rain-engulfed Wales. We've had a lovely time frolicking in the lake and barbecuing copious amounts of chicken, pig and cow. We've been to Budapest Zoo where we witnessed a reptilian orgy of Romanesque scale in the tortoise enclosure. We've ridden the child-slave railway through the mountains of Buda. We've drunk our body weights in Aperol Spritz. We've generated infantile chaos on the grandest of scales at some of the finest eateries that Budapest has to offer. It's been a blast, great to see them all and spend time together, and to see the cousins bond. But now I'm physically and mentally exhausted and wondering how anybody can cope with more than one child.

Before they leave, we visit an al fresco bar/restaurant. I look around. The children are off playing somewhere and my brother is also nowhere to be seen.

"Where's Ross?" I ask.

"I think he's behind that bush, somewhere over there?" replies his wife, Ceri.

"What's he doing behind a bush?"

Ceri just shrugs.

A few minutes later and Ross emerges carrying a plastic bag. Our eyes meet. Ross looks sad. He motions to the plastic bag. There's something in it.

"Pants." he says.

He sighs, looks straight ahead and walks a few more metres towards a bin. In the background his youngest then emerges from behind the same bush with a proud smile. Ross then turns to me, still looking sad.

"Diarrhoea." He says.

A few hours of pandemonium later and they have left. Mila is in bed and Zsuzsa and I are sitting in blissful silence on our sofa. I turn to my wife.

"Maybe I should get a vasectomy." I say.

"We should look into that." says Zsuzsa.